SUPPORT GROUP

Leader's Guide

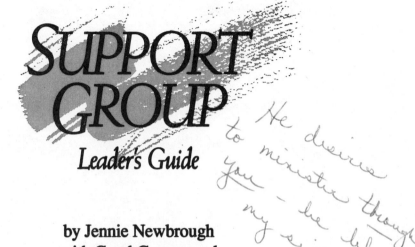

by Jennie Newbrough
with Carol Greenwood

A
LEADER'S
RESOURCE

A HEART ♥ ISSUES COMPANION

AGLOW.

Women's Aglow Fellowship Inte national
P.O. Box 1548
Lynnwood, WA 98046-1548
USA

Cover design by Technigraphic Systems, Inc.

ISBN 1-56616-005-7

1 2 3 4 5 Printing / Year 96 95 94 93

Contents

Section FIVE
KNOW YOUR SKILLS

Introduction and Acknowledgments

One late afternoon last October, I withdrew into the darkness of the living room hoping to escape into a nap.

Just a few hours earlier, I had received the final deadline date for this book from my Aglow editor, Karen Anderson. As I snuggled into the sofa and closed my eyes, I felt the nearness of the Lord.

"Lord," I whispered, "how can I finish this book to glorify You?"

I hadn't really expected an answer to the musing of my heart. But so softly He breathed, "Fill each page with the pounding of My heart . . . the pounding of My heart for redemption."

Warm tears washed my face as once again I beheld the heart of our Lord for each of us and for this book. How He loves us!

For the past three years I have been privileged by the Lord and by Women's Aglow Fellowship to serve as the U.S. support group resource person. Since then, I have been invited to share the vision and skills of support group ministry in local fellowships, area trainings, and Aglow retreats. My heart has been awed repeatedly as I have seen the Lord bring healing and light to hurting lives when I have shared His heart's desire for the body to minister one-to-another.

I give thanks to each Aglow board and every woman who received me and this ministry with love, enthusiasm, and joy. Your wise questions and open participation helped develop the material for this book. Most of all, your genuine loving response to this expression of ministry encourages me to continue sharing the vision.

To my family, John, Janna, and John, who accepted my many traveling weekends and endured my days in front of the word processor and my long distance hours on the phone with my coauthor, Carol Greenwood. To you who tolerated my messes throughout the house and my constant talking about "my book," thank you for allowing me to become who Christ has called me to be. Thank you for loving me this much. I so love you.

To my own personal Aaron and Ur, Clara Wilkins and Diane Moder, without whose abiding love, support, and prayers I would have given up on myself and this book long ago. Thank you for being all that Christ says a friend is to be. This book I dedicate to you both, for you have been *my* support group. I treasure you.

To the brave and steadfast U.S. fellowships department of WAF, thank you for sharing the vision and for totally supporting and upholding me with love and prayer. Susan Boucard, I have clung to your godly wisdom and loving guidance. Sharon Barrett and Susan, I love you and thank you for opening this door to me. And Deena Wilson, thank you for giving your keen eye and special touch to this manuscript.

To my counseling clients and support group participants who have consented to the use of your stories, thanks so much! I truly honor you. I have changed names and situations and am committed to guarding your confidence.

To Susan Goodnight who first "saw" this book, thank you for giving me life in so many ways. To Karen Anderson, dear patient and skilled editor and true encourager, thanks for laughter, joy, and confidence. And to Carol Greenwood, you have been an angel on assignment. How I thank God for you! I hold so dear what God has done between us.

I was asked how I was going to celebrate when this book was done. I paused to think. "What does celebration mean to me?" Immediately, I saw myself dancing in worship and praise before the Lord. So that is how I am going to celebrate! Please join me in worship and praise to a God who is able to do far above what we know to ask or think, to our Lord who is faithful to complete the good work He has begun, to the Father whose love is from everlasting to everlasting.

My prayer for you as you begin this book is that you will hear the pounding of God's heart for redemption and that your heart will beat in rhythm with His. May you be blessed by the privilege and challenge of the support group ministry.

To God be the glory!

Jennie Newbrough
June, 1993

A Special Note
to Aglow Leaders

Since the introduction of Aglow support groups in 1989, God has been powerfully using these compassionate "safe places" to transform the lives of countless women. In response to requests for more help in this dynamic area of ministry from you, our leaders, Aglow is introducing a new opportunity for existing and potential support group leaders.

In support group leadership we are touching some of the most intimate areas of women's lives. With this responsibility in mind, beginning in January 1994, each new Aglow support group leader must possess a Certificate of Completion awarded by the Aglow leadership. When you have finished reading this *Support Group Leader's Guide* and successfully completed the worksheets at the back of the book, you will be awarded your certificate. Existing Aglow support group leaders should begin to read and complete the worksheets as soon as possible.

We have made this book a special size with wide margins for your notes, in order to facilitate your learning and give you a chance to add your own thoughts.

All leaders' worksheets will be evaluated under the supervision of Aglow's support group resource person. For complete information on how to qualify for Aglow's support group Certificate of Completion, please see chapter 6, page 63 in this book. The "Perspective on Liability" which follows will tell you in more detail about the legal reasons for limiting Aglow's responsibility and authority in support group leadership.

It is Aglow's privilege to offer you this leadership development opportunity. May mended hearts, dried tears, and renewed hope for today's women be the reality and heritage of God's ministry through you.

Jennie Newbrough
Aglow Support Group Resource Person

Perspective
on Liability

This Aglow training material equips you to *support, comfort, listen, pray for,* and *examine* truth with those who come to Aglow support groups. This training *does not* equip you professionally in any way. You are cautioned *not* to give directive counsel, specific advice, or assume responsibility for someone's life in any way. To protect yourself from liability you must stay within the boundaries indicated.

Those of you who complete the worksheets in this book in order to receive a Certificate of Completion from Aglow must understand that doing so only allows you to lead an Aglow support group within the Aglow ministry.

When ministry peoples have been challenged in court, they have been vindicated because they did not hold themselves out to be licensed counselors, therapists, or other practicing professionals. Malpractice lawsuits only have validity against persons who regard themselves as professionals and have professional licenses to practice.

It is also important for liability protection that you refer those who need professional help to appropriate sources. We recommend that you keep a written record of any referrals, including the referral date.

Referral guidelines are given in section four, chapter 14 of this book.

Please make it known to your group that you are not acting in a professional role of any kind, that you will not counsel or give directive advice. You are their friend in Christ.

Section I

To Know God

THE PRIVILEGE of this section is to know God as He truly is and to minister His heart to those He came to seek and to save.

THE CHALLENGE of this section is to have His heart for one another and to fulfill our call as His Body to continue the healing, redeeming ministry of our Lord Jesus Christ.

1

...

The Adventure of Support Group Ministry

Those at this beginning place with support group ministry are very much like the pioneer women who braved the frontier. As my coauthor, Carol Greenwood, and I boarded the wagon of this adventure, we realized we approached pioneering quite differently.

Carol said, "Maybe it's my Pacific Northwest heritage or simply my natural curiosity about life, but I love adventure. Going new places, trying new food, and meeting new people energizes me. I love discovering the richness of life with all its variety and challenges. Undoubtedly, I would have made a good frontierswoman—if it weren't for the dust along the westward trail and the shortage of pizza parlors!

"Next to going on an adventure," Carol continued, "I like taking folks with me. Watching them discover something totally new to their life experience and seeing them challenged in new directions invigorates me as much as trailblazing ahead."

While Carol responded to the opportunity, I saw the challenge. I recalled crossing the Blue Ridge Mountains of

Virginia by car a few years ago and being awed at the thought of what it must have taken for the pioneer women to set out across those peaks without pavement or promise. Yet, it seems the call involved a commitment and courage that carried them on to possess the prize of new identity.

Carol and I have now walked a few miles in the support group "territory," learned a lot about the hills and valleys, the peaks and the plains of this ministry. And now, Carol, as a support group leader, and I, as Aglow's support group resource person, would like to bring you alongside in this venture.

We have discovered the powerful way God is using support groups to bring healing and wholeness to His Body. We have seen His Father's heart for hurting women in a way that makes us stand in awe at His tender love and mercy.

Good leaders, confident and well trained, are needed to carry this ministry forward. And since you're reading this book, I suspect you've already made the choice to "head out," to enlist in this wonderful adventure that touches so many women's lives with the grace and healing of the Lord Jesus.

I believe this *Support Group Leader's Guide* will be like a starting gun to get you motivated, like your right hand to feel your way along, like a road map to chart your direction, like your cheerleader when you hit a hard spot, and like your master question-answerer all along the way. Be assured that the Lord will be with you in this pursuit, for truly we have known His presence each step of the way.

I'm ready to move out. How about you?

LOOKING IN ON A SUPPORT GROUP

It is 7:30 on a Monday night and the group has gathered again at their usual place, Karen's family room. Linda and Marilyn are lying on the floor, their heads propped up against the front of the soft leather sofa. The rest, Ellen, Karen, Patty, and LuAnn have divided themselves among the remaining wingback chairs, hassocks, and rockers.

The group's bond is that each has recently experienced great loss. Marilyn and Lu are coping with divorce, Linda's home recently burned down, and Patty's toddler son was killed in a playground accident. Ellen's father died two months ago. Karen, the leader, lost her husband five years ago.

"Tonight we're going to talk about walls." Smiling and matter-of-fact, Karen leans forward, brushes a hand through her natural wavy hair, and opens the meeting. "Are any of you aware of building any walls as a result of your loss?"

Pausing, she looks around the room of thoughtful women. Then she continues, "When we've had loss, we often build walls as a result. In fact, I can give you a personal 'for instance.' When Jim died, it took me months before I would let another man touch me. Even when Dad wanted to hug me or just take my hand, I would pull back. I just didn't want to feel, so I denied myself the very comfort I needed. My wall really hurt me. It didn't protect me."

Linda shifts to an upright position. Tucking her legs to her side under a sofa pillow and smoothing out a wrinkle in her jeans, she speaks in a low voice. "Well, I have a wall and it's really hurting my family. I know Tim is frustrated with me. It's like I won't let my heart move into our new house. I haven't decorated or even done much cleaning."

"You really know where it hurts. I've got a wall a jack hammer couldn't break through." Marilyn reaches for a tissue. Then throwing her lap pillow to the floor, she emits a long sigh. "The worst of it is, I'm not sure I can ever pull it down or that I even want to. But I am in pain, I know that."

As each sees a wall of some type, Patty begins to weep. She finally breaks and lets her feelings out. "I have rejected my other children. I've pushed them away. I have been so selfish and so wrong. I don't want this wall. I want to hold my children again."

The evening speeds by as the women share honestly around the circle. There are tears, even some laughter.

Finally, Karen again poses a question as the time draws to a close. "You have said you were tired of your walls, can we make some choices tonight to love again?"

Quietly, each woman verbalizes her decision. The atmosphere is rich with acceptance. Love is tangible. God is healing. Hands joined, they gather in a circle and thank God for revealing truth and ask His strength to love again.

The women rise to sort out their purses, return their coffee cups to the kitchen, and retrieve their coats from the closet. No one really wants to leave. Finally, Linda says it all as she reaches for the front door handle, "Support group was good tonight."

SEEING THE HEART OF GOD

Was God at Karen's? Without a doubt He was there, listening, loving, and feeling the pain of these courageous women. Even more, I believe His heart is for their wholeness as He reveals the truth that sets them free. That's always been God's heart for His people—from Genesis to Revelation.

It is here, at this exact point, that we begin our instruction in leading support groups. This is the touchstone for all that flows out of this ministry:

To know God and to have God's heart for His people. This is the first challenge for any support group leader.

PERCEIVING THE FATHER'S HEART

Scripture is filled with graphic stories and illustrations of God's heart. We will be looking at these examples throughout this book. Our first example is a contemporary picture:

She slapped the note down on the kitchen counter, twirled around, and stormed out the door to the bus stop. Only two days before, this angry teenager had overwhelmed her mother and father with some seriously wrong behavioral choices.

This daughter had never done anything like this before

and her actions totally caught her parents by surprise. They were shocked—devastated. And now, to add to their pain, she had presented them with a personalized rejection scrawled across her lined notebook paper: "There's no way I want to live in this house any more with you. I'm moving into Judy's house. I can do what I want there."

Her mother, who'd read the note first, sank limply onto a stool at the kitchen counter, propping her head on her hands. Her feelings exploded into heavy weeping for ten or fifteen minutes. "Lord," she pleaded between sobs, "how do we handle this situation? I need your wisdom."

Within moments she identified an unmistakable voice, gently directed straight to her heart. "Give her what she needs, not what she deserves. Give her unconditional love."

The Lord's words quieted the anxious mother. Her tears stopped and she sat in silence, aware of a calming presence and the subsiding of the heavy tightness pressing in her chest.

Shortly the girl's broken-hearted father entered the kitchen, read the note, and spontaneously raged with his hurt. "Wait a minute here. I'm going to straighten out this young lady. I'm going to the school now." He grabbed his jacket from the back of a chair, dug for his car keys, and turned to walk out the kitchen door.

Bounding from the stool into her husband's path, the mother intervened. "No, wait! The Lord said to give her what she needs, not what she deserves. Give her unconditional love."

Their eyes locked in understanding as God's words filled the moment.

The father heard the Father.

He left for school with a different heart.

He asked to have his daughter excused from class and took her for a ride in the car where they could talk privately. As they drove along, weaving through the tree-studded suburban neighborhood, his words came like refreshing water from a gentle brook, "Honey, your mother and I want you to know that as of this moment, we start fresh. We totally forgive you as if nothing has happened. And we give you our total trust."

Later that afternoon, one bouncy teenage girl burst through the front door of her home, flung her backpack full of books across the kitchen counter and yelled, "Mom, I'm here. And I need a hug."

The Father's heart of love is amazing. To this family it brought healing and restoration. And more: it set a young girl free.

LOVE IN THE DESERT

Let's take another look at the Father's heart by backtracking several centuries to the barren desert east of Egypt. Here under the penetrating rays of the hot sun, we see a woman huddling by a spring just off the road to Shur. Such a picture of desolation. We can't help but ask ourselves what personal despair would have driven her to flee alone to the sunbaked desert.

Moving closer, we recognize the woman. She is Hagar. In her culture, names were rich indicators of character. Yet the name *Hagar* has no distinct meaning. Could this meaningless be part of her despair?

But wait, Hagar is not alone. Someone is speaking to her. Listen closely:

The angel of the Lord found Hagar. . . . and he said, "Hagar, servant of Sarai, where have you come from and where are you going?"

"I'm running away from my mistress Sarai," she answered.

Then the angel of the Lord told her, "Go back to your mistress and submit to her." The angel added, "I will so increase your descendants that they will be too numerous to count."

The angel of the Lord also said to her: "You are now with child and you will have a son. You shall name him Ishmael, for the Lord has heard of your misery. He will be a wild donkey of a man; his hand will be against everyone and everyone's hand against him, and he will live in hostility toward all his brothers."

She gave this name to the Lord who spoke to her: "You are the God who sees me," for she said, "I have now seen the One who sees me" (Gen. 16:7-12 NIV).

SEEING A VICTIM

In Hebrew the name for "the God who sees" is *Elroi*. What did God see? God saw more than a meaningless, sand-covered woman crouched by a bubbling spring. He saw a woman whom He knew by name. He saw her circumstances; he saw her misery. But, most significantly, He saw her future and her purpose.

Scripture tells us even more about Hagar. She was an Egyptian maidservant in the house of Abram and Sarai. This household, you will remember, was, by God's special promise, expecting to receive an heir. Even at their advanced ages, Abram and Sarai were to have a child. However, the years dragged by and no baby was conceived. Finally, in desperation, Sarai took matters into her own hands and made the decision to give Hagar to Abram so that a child might at least come from this union.

In simple terms, Sarai used Hagar to fulfill her own purposes to obtain a child. She never considered Hagar as a person, never acknowledged her feelings, desires, needs, or thoughts. By today's standards this seems unthinkable, yet it was an accepted custom in that time and culture.

Custom did not cancel feeling. Hagar knew she was being used. She was a woman with feelings and emotions, hopes and dreams of her own. But who cared? In her hurt, she despised Sarai.

Seeking to remain in control, Sarai complained to Abram about Hagar's attitude. Her husband reacted by giving Sarai permission to punish the very woman who carried his child. Poor Hagar, she now became the recipient of Abram's obvious disregard.

Most victims feel much like Hagar: "I don't matter." "No one cares." "I'm not important." And the next thought is: "I must get away from this place." That's precisely what Hagar did.

GOD IS NOT LIKE MAN

Elroi, the God who sees, saw Hagar so differently. Even though she was an Egyptian, and not of His people, she was known to Him. To Him she had significance and purpose. The God who saw Hagar did not rebuke her for despising Sarai nor did He chastise her for running away.

Instead, He saw *her*. He saw her pain, her needs, her circumstances. He gave her understanding, compassion, and hope. From her encounter with Elroi, Hagar received what the Prophet Jeremiah talked about years later—a future and a hope (See Jeremiah 29:11). She could now lift her head, return home, and fulfill the purpose God had for her life.

Later, in Genesis 21, we again find Elroi delivering Hagar from despair. Sarah complained to Abraham (by now God had changed their names) that Hagar's son, Ishmael, was mocking Isaac and succeeded in getting Abraham to order the mother and son out of the house, to fend for themselves.

Weeping over the prospects of losing her son to thirst in the hot desert, Hagar is again visited by Elroi. This time God comes with the provision of fresh water and a promise to make Ishmael into a great nation.

God is faithful to see. He had a covenant with Abraham to bless his seed—and He did not revoke it; Ishmael was Abraham's seed. God has a covenant through Christ to redeem our lives. Just as God opened Hagar's eyes to see Him, He desires to be seen by those who are hurt and confused today. Support groups can be those wells of refuge to which victims flee to find the God who sees and fulfills His covenant.

THE POUNDING OF GOD'S HEART

Hagar's story reflects the heart of God for hurting people. His heart of mercy, compassion, and justice. His heart that regards every person with love and significance. Our understanding of support group ministry begins here.

The heartbeat of God pounds with love for His precious creation. The Bible, in fact, has often been called a "love letter" from the Father to His children. Over 600 years before Christ, the prophet Isaiah conveyed God's love in language so powerful that to this day it stirs us to awesome amazement as He describes the purpose of sending His Son in our behalf. Listen again to the majestic proclamation:

> The Lord has anointed me to preach good news to the poor. . . . to bind up the brokenhearted . . . to proclaim freedom for the captives and release . . . for the prisoners, to proclaim the year of the Lord's favor and the day of vengeance of our God, to comfort all who mourn, and provide for those who grieve . . . to bestow on them a crown of beauty instead of ashes, the oil of gladness instead of mourning, and a garment of praise instead of a spirit of despair. . . . For I, the Lord, love justice; I hate robbery and iniquity. . . . For Zion's sake I will not keep silent . . . till her righteousness shines out the dawn. . . . No longer will they call you Deserted, or name your land Desolate. . . . You will be called Hephzibah [my delight is in her] . . . for the Lord will take delight in you and your land will be married. . . . As a bridegroom rejoices over his bride, so will your God rejoice over you. . . . They will be called the Holy People, The Redeemed of the Lord; and you will be called Sought After, the City No Longer Deserted (Isa. 61:1-3, 8, 62:1, 4, 5, 12 NIV).

Do you hear the pounding of God's heart?

JESUS' JOB DESCRIPTION

In the fullness of time, Jesus Himself stood in the synagogue in Nazareth. To announce His mission, He read a portion of these words from Isaiah and then added, "Today this scripture is fulfilled in your hearing." Luke records that his hearers were startled by His gracious words (See Luke 4:21).

This job description is just as arresting today, perhaps not so much because of the messianic implication that Jesus represented to His Jewish hearers but more from the simple fact that as humans our tendency is to turn away from those who mourn, those in shame, those suffering grief, devastation, and disgrace. Not so our Lord! He came for the very purpose of embracing mankind in these humbled conditions in order to impart His life and redemption.

We see Christ display this heart on behalf of the woman caught in adultery (John 8). We see Jesus turn aside to give a Samaritan woman a drink of eternal life (John 4). We see Him release healing virtue as a woman's hand of faith merely touched His garment (Luke 8:43-48).

This love so graphically illustrated in the life of Jesus, love that sees the person beneath the circumstances, is the heart of God that is necessary for support group ministry.

OUR JOB DESCRIPTION

We, the Body of Christ, are to carry on the work of Christ through His Holy Spirit. His job description becomes ours.

As the Body of Christ we are to minister to the brokenhearted, those captive, those mourning, those grieving, those in shame, those in disgrace, those devastated, those ruined, those robbed, those in iniquity, those deserted, those desolate.

As the Body of Christ we are to minister the Good News, the favor of the Lord, beauty, gladness, the vengeance of the Lord, His reward, His recompense, His redemption, His restoration.

As the Body of Christ we are to embrace others when they are in these not-so-lovely places. We are to impart the love, mercy, compassion, and healing of Christ.

This is the challenge that pounds in our hearts—a ministry that embraces the Father's heart! That's what Aglow support groups are all about.

2

...

"One Anothering"

When Aglow first considered establishing suppor. groups, many people expressed genuine concerns and questions.

Is there really a need for these kinds of groups? Aren't Bible study groups sufficient as places of ministry? How do these groups become a part of the Aglow "network of caring women"?

To give answers to these questions, Aglow held a panel discussion on support groups during the 1990 international conference in Washington, D.C.

As part of that panel, I was asked to answer the question: "What is the greatest need for women today?" The question seemed too big for me; I felt small and inadequate to answer.

I sought God for His answer, much like a persistent two-year-old child pulling on Daddy's trousers. "Father," I pressed, "what do you see as the greatest need of women today?" His answer came with impact when He impressed me with the story of the Samaritan woman in John 4.

THE MESSAGE OF THE SAMARITAN WOMAN

I could almost see her across the barriers of time and culture: the Samaritan woman with a tarnished reputation, hurting in her isolation and pain. Just an ordinary woman pressed by her past to endure the scorching rays of the midday sun to fetch a jug of water at the well. An ordinary woman who met Jesus and gave Him a drink of water.

However, this Jewish man was unlike any man she'd ever met. He accepted her. In exchange for her shame, her hopelessness, her interminable search for love, Jesus offered her the water of eternal life. The Lord used this familiar story to impress me that His desire to minister to women is still the same: to extend His Father's heart of acceptance, love, and healing.

And where are these women? Probably not walking around dressed in sandals and long robes, balancing water jugs on their heads like the woman at Jacob's well. But they are everywhere.

They live next door, they jog past you in the park, brush against you in the express elevator of the downtown office building, and hand you your prescription from the pharmacy. The cumulative effects of dysfunctional homes, divorces, abuse, addictions, compulsions, financial stress, and multiple role expectations have gripped the lives of countless millions of women, imprisoning them in hopelessness, isolation, shame, depression, and fear.

These women desperately need compassionate understanding of where they are and why, and hope for a way out of their pain. Their hearts are closed and their spirits wounded. And the good news is that this same Christ wants to reach out to them, through you and me.

We are His arms. Through His Body we can enfold hurting women with understanding, love, and hope. Support groups offer this unique opportunity for a woman to come out of her pain, through her victimization, to live in the glorious freedom of a godly woman. Without a doubt, this is another way Aglow can fulfill the call to be a "network of caring women."

CALLED TO "ONE ANOTHER"

Throughout His life and His Word, Christ has called us to love one another. His clarion call to "one anothering" will resound perpetually throughout the world until He returns.

Let's search out for a moment what it means to "one-another" one another. Scripture exhorts us with a powerful list:

- Comfort one another
- Bear one another's burdens
- Love one another
- Fellowship one with another
- Minister one to another
- Confess your faults one to another
- Forgive one another
- Submit one to another
- Be kind one to another
- Prefer one another
- Pray one for another
- Have compassion one to another

In the New Testament alone there are over fifty references to "one anothering." These admonitions only confirm the heart of God's divine wisdom for His people.

From the beginning God planned for His people to live in relationship. He makes that clear early in Genesis: "It is not good that man should be alone" (Gen. 2:18). God's plan for relationship is for interdependence in relationship to Him and one another. His plan is that we would both give and receive one from the other, having first received Him.

Consider what the preacher in the book of Ecclesiastes had to say about the effect of "one anothering":

Two are better than one, because they have a good reward for their labor. For if they fall, one will lift up his companion. But woe to him who is alone when he falls, for he has no one to help him up. Again, if two lie down together, they will keep warm; but how can one be warm alone? (Eccles. 4:9-12).

INDIVIDUALISTIC THINKING IS DECEPTIVE

The devil's deception always runs counter to God's intent. It is Satan himself who has deceived us with humanistic thinking that we should "do things ourselves," "handle our own problems," "stand on our own two feet." This individualistic approach to life never issued from the mind and heart of God.

Sadly, too many Christians have accepted the deception of the enemy and feel embarrassed or ashamed if they need help. Or when they acknowledge their need for help they are rebuked by some part of the Body for "not having enough faith," "not praying enough," "having sin in your life." When this happens, the Body ministers condemnation to itself rather than the support Christ ordained.

GOOD NEWS ON AN AIRPLANE

Because I was so intent on knowing that the concept of support groups was solidly biblical, I continually dug in Scripture.

In fact I was doing this on a flight between Louisiana and Pennsylvania, my Bible in hand and my tea on the tray in front of me. Paging through the opening chapters of Ephesians in the New International Version, I suddenly found the lost treasure.

My heart leaped there in the skies over the middle of the United States. I proclaimed my joy aloud: "Yes! Yes! *Support* is in God's Word—right there in the book of Ephesians."

Paul's words set the course for relationships in the Body of Christ:

To prepare God's people for works of service, so that the body of Christ may be built up until we can all reach unity in the faith and in the knowledge of the Son of God and become mature, attaining to the whole measure of the fullness of Christ (Eph. 4:12-13 NIV).

You can't help but feel the emphasis on presenting a vibrant Christ to the world. But, what does this involve? Nothing short of believers choosing to grow up. Paul goes on:

Then we will no longer be infants, tossed back and forth by the waves, and blown here and there by every wind of teaching and by the cunning and craftiness of men in their deceitful scheming. Instead, speaking the truth in love, we will in all things grow up into him who is the Head, that is, Christ (Eph. 4:14-15 NIV).

Paul proceeds to unveil his powerful analogy of the human body. We can't miss his point:

From him the whole body joined and held together by every supporting ligament, grows and builds itself up in love, as each part does its work" (Eph. 4:16 NIV).

Hallelujah! Here was the irrefutable evidence I wanted. Without a doubt, it is God's plan that we join ourselves *one-to-another* that the whole Body of Christ will grow up into Him.

WE ARE TO BE SUPPORTING LIGAMENTS

In this passage the New International Version of the Bible uses the term "supporting ligaments" where other versions use "joints."

A little anatomy lesson helps us. It is the ligaments that are essential to the joint being a joint. Ligaments join the bones together. Do you see their necessity? Without ligaments the body would fall apart, collapse in a heap!

With ligaments, we can stand erect, assume other positions, and most importantly, *move*.

Now look at the parallel in the Body of Christ. When there are no supporting ligaments, the Body moves independently in directions God never intended. Paul has a phrase for it: "Tossed to and fro . . . with every wind of doctrine" (See Ephesians 4:14). When we are not properly joined to the Body, we remain immature and do not grow up in Christ Jesus. Or in the worst case scenarios, the Body collapses and simply becomes ineffective for the Lord. .

Let yourself picture God motivated by His divine affection for us. Capture the image of His plan: His Body—strong, mature, and fully joined to Christ, moving with wisdom, truth, and power under His headship.

CALLED TO EPHESIANS 4 MINISTRY

Support groups offer a place for this Ephesians 4 ministry to happen—and to flourish. Let me tell you about Nancy, who benefited from this ministry.

A victim of childhood abuse, Nancy had sought professional Christian counseling. The sessions were productive and she was doing well, opening herself up to God's healing for the years of damage she'd encountered. Yet when she joined a local Aglow support group her healing was accelerated.

Earlier in her healing process Nancy shared with me that whenever she was with people she felt as if there were a glass wall separating her from others. On one side, people were laughing and talking and enjoying life. She, however, was stuck on the other side, alone, unable to pass through and be a part of the group. Obviously these feelings of isolation caused her much anguish.

Nancy felt "safe" in the loving atmosphere of the support group. Because of the shared feelings of others, she felt free to enter in and share her pain. For the first time in her life she didn't have to hide or struggle with feeling different.

Through individual counseling and the comfort of the

support group, she has passed through what felt like an impenetrable wall. Her personal relationship with God has blossomed; she has come into a genuine experience of the Father's love for her, something which eluded her for years. Now alive with the love of Christ, she is an officer for her local Aglow chapter and is also leading an Aglow support group for abuse victims.

FREE TO RECEIVE, FREE TO GIVE

What happened to bring about all the healing in Nancy? Nothing more and nothing less than Ephesians 4 ministry: In love, truth was spoken, prayer was made, faults were confessed, forgiveness extended, and comfort dispensed. And the results? A hurting, wounded woman became healed and restored to love again.

Nancy's story accurately illustrates the profound effect "one anothering" can have on our lives. Once, others in the Body were support for her, and now she is strength for others.

The marvel of God's ways! Healing love is like hair mousse: release a small amount and it envelopes everything it touches. We are "lathered" with His grace (See Ephesians 1:8). Jesus said, "Freely you have received, freely give" (Matt. 10:8).

3
...

God's Beauty Shop

From the beginning of time, God ordained life to be a series of processes. I often forget this fact. Like a couple of months ago when I experienced a "foot and finger tapping" kind of day.

You know that kind? From the moment I opened my eyes in the morning, I thought, "Oh, no, there won't be enough hours in this day to get everything done." I didn't even have to consult my calendar to know this would be a jammed up, live-on-the-run day. So I ignored the dog's wet nose pushed lovingly at my pillow, skipped my slippers, and hit the floor running.

Breakfast was a mere fleeting thought as I revved the car engine and pulled out of the driveway, drawn like a robot to a demanding schedule. All the while one thought flashed across my mind: *Hurry up*! It was so vivid I was convinced the whole world saw it in red neon letters.

Impatience invades even the simplest activities on this kind of day. Like waiting in line at McDonald's. Or standing at the check-out counter while the grocery clerk calls for a price check. Meanwhile, what am I doing to occupy myself with in this interlude? Enjoying a mini-vacation? No, not me. I'm tapping my foot or running my fingers across the counter like a musician practicing her scales in double time, all the time wishing these folks would hurry up!

Most of us become frustrated when things in our lives take time and involve a process. We are a results-oriented society. The sooner, the better. And *now* is preferable.

No wonder we are stressed and uncomfortable with this pace and agenda. It was never meant to be.

GOD'S WAY INVOLVES PROCESS

Almost everything we do in relation to God involves a process, whether it's salvation, baptism, worship, redemption, restoration, prayer, healing, or sanctification.

Even creation didn't happen with one God-orchestrated note. It was a seven-day symphony! Creation was the first recorded process, giving birth to all other processes that humans would engage in: life, death, love, birth, work, planting, harvesting, eating, and sleeping.

However, when these processes seem to take too long in our lives, we have a tendency to balk. While we're digging in our heels, there are believers who insist that everything that needed doing was taken care of at the time of salvation or baptism and that there is no need to "go through all that."

They want to see people go to the altar, receive prayer, and "be all better." The times at the altar and the times of prayer are but steps on the road to God's process in our lives.

We want life's processes to be fast and preferably painless. In this age of instant coffee and instant potatoes, microwave dinners, and fast cash, we also want "quick fixes" in our spiritual and emotional lives.

If only we could slow down and listen to the calm assurance of Paul as he reminded the believers at Philippi: "He who began a good work in you will carry it to completion until the day of Christ Jesus" (Phil. 1:6).

When we resist the processes of God, we often deny ourselves the very things we seek—healing, deliverance, restoration, wholeness, love, joy, peace, and righteous-ness. Why would we deny ourselves these precious things?

Ah, there is an easy answer: the word *process* means *change*. And we all fear change. It throws us out of our comfort zones, catapults us out of the driver's seat of our lives, and we feel like we are careening out of control. Being out of control is uncomfortable; it's threatening to the way we've run our lives. Thus we pull back from any process that invites change.

IT TAKES COURAGE TO CHANGE

As an ordained minister I work as a Christian counselor, and I realize that the bravest people in the world walk through the doors of my office. They usually enter timid, angry, doubtful, ashamed, fearful, or discouraged; but in God's eyes they are courageous.

It takes courage to face change. In the eyes of much of the world and too much of the Christian family, those who seek help to change are considered weak. But the Lord sees them differently. He sees them as seekers after Him-self, people bravely pursuing His faithfulness. He moves strongly to come alongside to help them, and rewards them with His righteousness and redemption.

These are the people who will come to your support groups. They may not appear or sound brave at all, but by taking the initial step to join a support group they have signaled their intent to enter a process that will involve facing the dreaded monster: *change*. It is vitally important, therefore, that you see support group members the way the Lord sees them: *courageous*. Come alongside as God does and cheer them on with your encouragement and hope. You may even have to exhort them to remain committed to change as much as Paul had to exhort the churches and Timothy:

Pursue righteousness, godliness, faith, love, patience, gentleness. Fight the good fight of faith, lay hold on eternal life to which you were also called and have confessed the good confession (1 Tim. 6:11, 12).

GETTING READY FOR A WEDDING

The God of processes is wonderfully portrayed in Deuteronomy:

> When you go to war against your enemies . . . and you take captives, if you notice among the captives a beautiful woman and are attracted to her, you may take her as your wife. Bring her into your home and have her shave her head, trim her nails, and put aside the clothes she was wearing when captured. After she has . . . mourned her father and mother for a full month, then you may go to her and be her husband and she shall be your wife (Deut. 21:10-13).

Clearly this is the process of preparing a bride. All the details are spelled out. Now look at the New Testament parallel. It is a striking comparison:

The Lord Jesus Christ is also claiming a bride. He went to battle against His enemy and has chosen a bride from the inhabitants of the land.

This bride, the Body of Christ, is in a similar process. In a figurative way, the Lord has asked us to shave our heads. Or in other words, to exchange the glory of the world for the glory of the Lord. He has called for us to trim our nails—to submit our self-sufficiency and need to control. And we have been asked to put off the old garments of our natural life and put on the new nature of Christ.

SUPPORT GROUPS CAN BE GOD'S BEAUTY SHOP

Any woman who has been "done up" in a beauty shop can tell you that in the process of beautifying with perm rods, mud masks, bleaches, drying, cutting, toning, brushing, curling, moussing, spraying—she often looks worse than when she came in.

She is in the humbling state of becoming undone to be redone. It is common for beauticians to hear intimate details of a customer's life. Somehow trust is created because the beautician is bringing forth beauty in the client's life. This sets the stage for openness and vulnerability.

In the same way, support groups can be God's beauty shops for the soul. If group members believe you have a vision of beauty for their lives, trust will enable openness and vulnerability to lead to change.

Remember the previous reference of support groups as safe places? I believe we need safe places to be "shaved, clipped, and stripped." It is in a support group that the bride adorns herself with the "fine linen" provided her. Support groups become God's beauty shop where the Holy Spirit, working through the Body of Christ, helps the bride make herself ready.

This speaks of a process of change in which the bride must actively and willfully participate. Each person coming to your support group will grow and change only to the degree she participates in her own process of change. Your task as the group leader is to provide the "dressing room" or the "beauty shop," but each person must choose to change.

THREE STAGES OF CHANGE

In support groups we present three stages of change. We help people become

- Aware of their thinking, feelings, and behaviors
- Responsible for their feelings, behaviors, decisions
- Free to know God, free to serve, free to love, free to witness, free to live as godly women

Melinda Fish, in her book *Adult Children and the Almighty,* writes: "For many people, being born again has brought a great sense of relief from the sins of the past, but it has failed to heal the wounds they suffered."[1]

Ps. 23 - He restoreth my soul (handwritten)

Her book emphasizes the restoration ministry of Christ in our lives and points to the Good Shepherd and His desire to restore our soul. She goes on to say, "I did not know that a person's unresolved past stifles his joy and smothers his Christian life as much as the grave clothes would have smothered Lazarus if he had not been set free from them."[2]

Another author, Edwin Cole, points to our need for change in a little different way. In *Maximized Manhood* he writes: "We don't talk about sins today, we talk about problems. The reason that problems are more convenient than sins is that we don't have to do anything about problems. If you only have a problem, you can get sympathy for it or understanding for it or you can get professional help for it, to name a few.

"Sins, on the other hand, have to be repented of, confessed, and forsaken. All problems in life are somehow based on sin. That's why Jesus Christ came to die for our sins, and be the answer to all our problems."[3]

Both of these authors address the basic elements that take place in the three stages of change just mentioned.

BECOMING AWARE

We must become aware of the wounds in our lives and open to the restoration process of Christ. We cannot nurse our wounds and use them as an excuse for un-Christlike behavior, such as timidity, aggressiveness, compulsions, rages, withdrawal, etc. Neither should we try to repress our wounds, for they fester in the behaviors and feelings we display anyway.

In 1 Corinthians 13:10-11, Paul explains a profound truth:

When I was a child, I talked like a child, I thought like a child, I reasoned like a child. When I became a man, I put childish ways behind me.

When the wounds of childhood are not healed, we continue to live emotionally at the age of this wounded child— we cannot grow up. But, when we become aware, then we can take responsibility to seek healing for this child within.

Denial is just another form of bondage. We must become aware of our feelings, actions, and thoughts that come from our woundedness so that we can cooperate with Christ's restoration work in our lives.

BECOMING RESPONSIBLE

Once we are aware and are receiving healing, we can then become responsible for ourselves, no longer blaming the past, and entering into the repentance, confession, and forsaking that Dr. Cole addresses.

When a person is victimized by life, she, often without conscious knowledge, becomes what I call "a victim of being a victim." She thinks and responds to life situations as a victim all the time. She usually would not think of this as sinful behavior, but it is.

You will encounter this in your groups, particularly at first. Let me give you an example. As the middle child in an alcoholic home, Sheila was emotionally abused. Now with three children, married to a gentle, loving husband, she will not ask him to help with things around the house, even when she is overwhelmed.

She says, "Oh, Jim will think I'm lazy and besides he works hard on the job." The truth is that Jim has never said she was lazy. That was what she heard from her father. In fact, Jim has expressed a desire to share things with her. But she brushes him off saying she can manage.

Playing the martyr role, Sheila is denying herself the help she needs, plus putting up a wall between herself and her husband. She is living as the victim of abuse even though that abuse took place long ago. Would Sheila consider it sinful behavior? Probably not. But it is. She is failing to be open and honest and, therefore, is unloving in her relationships.

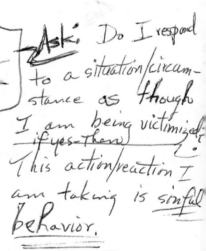

Ask: Do I respond to a situation/circumstance as though I am being victimized? if yes—Then: This action/reaction I am taking is sinful behavior.

BECOMING FREE

A support group could well be Sheila's ticket to freedom. Here she could become aware that her behavior is coming from her past. She would be challenged to take responsibility to risk, to ask for help, and to begin thinking and reacting in new ways. Becoming open and vulnerable to help, she will eventually be free to simply be herself and express her needs honestly. She will be well on her way to enjoying the "togetherness" of her marriage in an atmosphere that is truly loving.

Our great and merciful God understands the processes of life and the effects of change. Through Christ, He gives the grace to change. We, as His Body, provide the encouragement.

It is a privilege to work in God's beauty shop. It is a challenge to understand the processes of change and to help His chosen people through them.

Paul says it so well when he describes our hope:

Being transformed into his likeness with ever-increasing glory, which comes from the Lord who is the Spirit" (2 Cor. 3:18 NIV).

4

...

Knowing God as He Truly Is

Because the bruises of life often color our concept of God, it is imperative as support group leaders that we know what Scripture says and that we accurately convey this truth to those in our groups. A brush with a harsh father, negative experiences from an authority figure, or even the grief of losing a precious loved one can distort our picture of what God is really like. Take Carla's experience, for example.

When she was only five years old her mother became emotionally ill and was hospitalized in a state institution several hours from the family home. At the same time, Carla's father's job took him away for two or three weeks at a time on engineering projects in a neighboring state. Left in the care of an aged great-grandmother, Carla and her brother often felt abandoned and uncared for.

Grandmother was too tired to read bedtime stories to the children, too tired to toss the ball or even have other children over to play dress-up or hide and seek. No one affirmed the little drawings Carla brought home from school or gave her a hug when she left in the morning. Even when she fell playing in the yard, her grandmother scolded her for being clumsy rather than embracing her, drying her tears, and quieting her frightened heart.

Finally, after their parents' divorce, the children were sent to live on their grandparents' farm where, they at last experienced more stability. However, by this time, the self-protective walls were already in place, covering the hurts that were never allowed expression.

Repeatedly Carla's father promised to come to his daughter's piano recital, her school play, or even graduation, but more often than not, he broke the promise when last minute business took priority over his daughter's life.

Years later, Carla went to her pastor for counseling because she struggled so intensely with feelings of abandonment. Taught in church and Sunday school that God loved her unconditionally, she, nevertheless, couldn't silence her underlying fears that He couldn't be depended upon. Experiences told her He was too tired or too busy to care. Fortunately, with the help of a godly pastor and Scripture, she was able to forgive the past and come to a true understanding of who her Heavenly Father really is.

Many women coming to support groups can relate to Carla's experience. Without a true comprehension of God, they will remain emotionally and spiritually crippled. Deep healing at the heart level will elude them.

PICTURE OF THE UNCHANGING GOD

Imagine God calling you up to make an appointment. He has something on His mind He wants to discuss with you, namely to let you know a little more about Himself. Minus the telephone, that's pretty much how He approached Moses in Exodus 34:

> The Lord said to Moses, "Chisel out two stone tablets like the first ones, and I will write on them the words that were on the first tablets, which you broke. Be

ready in the morning, and then come up on Mount Sinai (Ex. 34: 1-3 NIV).

Moses, indeed kept the appointment. He climbed the mountain, alone as instructed, carrying the stone tablets in his arms.

Punctual as usual, the Lord came down in a cloud and stood before Moses to proclaim His name. Then, in an incredible once-only gesture, He passed in front of Moses with a bold pronouncement:

The Lord, the Lord, the compassionate and gracious God, slow to anger, abounding in love and faithfulness, maintaining love to thousands, and forgiving wickedness, rebellion and sin. Yet He does not leave the guilty unpunished (Ex. 34:6-7 NIV).

What a self-portrait of the God of the universe—God's own voice announcing Himself in unambiguous terms. Before Moses, passed God's heart, His character, His nature, His very essence. What an awesome experience! No wonder Moses bowed to the ground and worshipped Him.

God is unchanging. He is the same yesterday, today, and forever. What He was to Moses and His people in the wilderness, He is for you and those who come to your support group.

LETTING THE WORD OF GOD BE OUR SOURCE

This challenge—to know God as He truly is—is absolutely essential to our helping others. This is not static knowledge; it is ever unfolding as the Holy Spirit continues to reveal the Word of God to us. Paul, a great student of the Scriptures, underscores the vastness of this truth:

Oh, the depth of the riches both of the wisdom and knowledge of God! How unsearchable are His judgments, and His ways past finding out! For who has known the mind of the Lord? Or who has become His counselor? (Rom. 11:33-34).

As support group leaders, we must be willing to let the Word of God be our source of understanding of Him. We must let go of our biases, our past understanding, even our own feelings about God or any other source that does not line up with Scripture. *The Word of God is our basis for presenting who God is.*

CONSIDER THE PEANUT BUTTER JAR LID

I was at an Aglow retreat in Pennsylvania sharing on the importance of having a correct concept of God when the Lord gave me an unusual vision—my peanut butter jar. I have a habit of screwing jar lids on crooked, so I immediately realized what He was pointing out. For years, my husband has called my attention to this problem. It seemed like such a minor thing to me. So, quite frankly, I dismissed his comments, thinking he had the problem. After all, I reasoned, at least the lid was on the jar and not lost!

But the Lord got my attention and I learned something. When the lid is crooked, air comes in and when air comes in bacteria and contamination distort and steal the purity, freshness, and aroma of the peanut butter. Consequently, the essence of the peanut butter is lost.

The Lord had made His point. When our spiritual "lids" are on crooked, the truth of God's heart for us is contaminated by the enemy, the prince of the air. We are left with a distortion of God that changes our relationship with Him.

TRUTH WILL SET US FREE

In John's Gospel, Jesus promises that we "shall know the truth and the truth shall make you free" (John 8:32). Many today are not free to live godly lives simply because they do not know the truth of God's heart for them.

As support group leaders we need to have our spiritual "lids" on straight so we can help others know the truth.

This is their road to freedom. While we realize that no one totally knows God, it is our responsibility as leaders to present Him as His Word reveals Him and, at the same time, to be ever growing in our own knowledge of Him through His Word.

Many who come to your groups will be like Carla. They will *not* have their "lids on straight." A variety of things could have affected their concept of God:

- Childhood thinking, personal opinion
- Self-image, life experiences
- Personal temperament, parental messages
- Church teachings, doctrinal beliefs
- Satanic lies, media messages, etc.

Change does not happen overnight. It took time to develop these wrong concepts and it will take time and patience to get rid of them. Some in your groups may struggle with letting go of long held erroneous beliefs. As the leader you are not to argue or demand change, but simply to lay the foundation that God's Word is the group's only basis for determining truth and knowing God.

This is one of the reasons we recommend Aglow *Heart Issues* books or Aglow-approved material be used in support groups. These materials convey a correct concept of God and lay the foundation of truth that is needed for healing and change.

QUESTIONS AS PRIMARY TOOLS

As a leader you will quickly become sensitive to comments that group members make about God. When you hear someone say something like, "I know I will never please God," or "I know I deserve to be punished by the Lord," you know that God is being wrongly represented and that truth needs to replace the wrong belief.

What is the best way to handle these kinds of negative comments? I recommend the primary tool of support group leadership: *questions*. I ask questions and keep asking questions.

Questions draw out the truth from within the person. Rather than telling the person truth, as the leader you can help her discover truth for herself.

I often have the woman open a Bible and read the truth that applies to the particular aspect of God under discussion. I found this to be effective for both Christians and non-Christians.

HOW TO USE QUESTIONS (AN EXAMPLE)

The following dialogue between Susan (fictitious) and her support group leader illustrates how using questions can help a person discover truth:

Susan: I just know I will never please God.

S.G.L.:   Many people feel that way.

Susan: Why does God make it so hard?

S.G.L.:   Are you aware of any scriptures that have those answers?

Susan: When I read the Word, all I see are the verses that list my sins.

S.G.L.:   I've got my Bible open to one that says a lot to me. Will you read it to me?

Susan: Okay. Well, I know this scripture. It's John 3:16, 17. "For God so loved the world that he gave his one and only Son, that whoever believes in him shall not perish but have eternal life. For God did not send his Son into the world to condemn the world, but to save the world through him" (NIV).

S.G.L.:   Susan, have you accepted Jesus as your Savior?

Susan: Yes, you know that.

S.G.L.:   Then is God pleased with you? Has He given you eternal life?

Susan: Well, yes, but . . . (Give her time to reflect).

S.G.L.:   Did God send His Son to condemn you?

Susan: It says, "No."

S.G.L.:   According to this scripture, why did God send Christ to die? (Pause. This is a moment of truth.)

Susan: Well, it says because He loves me. You mean God isn't mad at me? That He loves me?

S.G.L.:   Yes, Susan, God loves you. He even says His love is unconditional and nothing can separate you from His love.

This process of asking questions helps the members of the group begin to think with biblical truth as their plumb line, rather than simply going by their feelings. Feelings, while important, can be deceptive and without truth; they can hold us in bondage. Questions asked with gentleness and sensitivity are a wonderful tool to challenge us to think and thus discover truth for ourselves.

SCRIPTURES THAT REVEAL THE HEART OF GOD

As a support group leader you will do well to have an arsenal of scriptures available which clearly reveal God's heart. Consider the following as a starter list:

• Cast your cares on the Lord and he will sustain you; he will never let the righteous fall (Ps. 55:22 NIV).

• The eyes of the Lord are on the righteous and His ears are open to their cry. . . . The righteous cry out, and the Lord hears, and delivers them out of all their troubles. The Lord is near to those who have a broken heart, and saves such as have a contrite spirit (Ps. 34:15-18).

• Praise be to the God and Father of our Lord Jesus Christ, the Father of compassion and the God of all comfort, who comforts us in all our troubles so that we can comfort those in any trouble with the comfort we ourselves have received from God (2 Cor. 1: 3-5 NIV).

• We do not have a high priest who is unable to sympathize with our weaknesses, but we have one who has been tempted in every way, just as we are—yet, was without sin. Let us then approach the throne of grace with confidence, so that we may receive mercy and find grace to help us in our time of need (Heb. 4:15-16 NIV).

These scriptures reveal the compassionate, caring, comforting heart of God. People in places of pain or change need to hear this truth in order to trust Him.

AN EXERCISE IN EXAMINING OUR LIDS

Remember what God taught me through the peanut butter jar with the crooked lid?

As support group leaders we need to constantly examine our "lids." We do this by searching God's Word and lining it up with our beliefs. Using the scriptures from the previous list, let's try a little exercise that will challenge and prepare you to help those in your support groups.

Scripture: Hebrews 4:15-16
Questions: What is God feeling toward us when we are tempted?
                What does He want to give us?
                Is He angry with us?
                Does He condemn us and tell us we should be ashamed?
Comment: If your "lid" is on crooked, you will think God is angry and perhaps that being tempted is a sin. You may think you have to be strong in yourself to earn God's love and approval. Truth says that Christ understands the power of temptation and that He desires to give us the mercy and grace that enable Him to overcome so that we, through Him, may overcome. He desires

to help us, not judge us.

Scripture: 2 Corinthians 1: 3-5
Questions: When you have troubles, what does God
                say He will do for you? How easily do you
                receive this from Him? When your troubles
                don't go away, do you think that God
                doesn't love you or that He is punishing
                you? What type of father is God?
Comment: People often have their minds made up as
                to what God should do for them and so do
                not receive His comfort. We often think
                God is like our natural fathers and do not
                see Him as compassionate toward us.

Scripture: Psalm 34: 15-18
Questions: Does God hear our cries? Will He respond?
                Whose cries does the Lord hear?
Comment: Often we are self-reliant and do not call on
                God. We must be honest when life hurts
                and willing to cry out to God. People
                frequently complain against God when life
                is difficult rather than cry out to Him.

These scriptures, questions, and comments were given
to encourage you to lay aside past teachings and opinions
and read what the Word actually says.

I once heard Pastor Robert Cornwall share a tip for
keeping God's truth fresh to his heart. He said he gets a
new, unmarked Bible each year so that he is not relying on
past insight into the Word; thus he is always open to what
the Spirit is saying. I am not suggesting that you get a new
Bible but that you be open to reviewing your concepts
about God in light of His Word, anew and afresh.

I have yet to talk with a support group leader who has
not found "crooked lids" in her group. Be assured that
you, too, will encounter this challenge when you lead a

support group. Therefore be prepared with a gentle attitude—you will want to present God as He truly is.

You have now completed the reading in Section One. Please
turn to the worksheets for this section on page 203, and reproduce a copy. Then fill in your answers on the copy. If you are
applying to become an Aglow support group leader, mail your
completed sheets to Jennie Newbrough at the address on page
202. Be sure to include a stamped, self-addressed, business
size (#10) envelope to facilitate their return. If you are reading for
your own edification, you also may want to reproduce the
worksheets, fill them in, and keep them as part of your self-study.

Section II
To Know Yourself

THE PRIVILEGE of this section is to see and appreciate yourself as the unique creation of God that you are and to become aware of the ways He has gifted you for the work of His service.

THE CHALLENGE of this section is to evaluate yourself honestly and become responsible to grow and change so that your ministry for the King will bear much good fruit.

5

...

The Calling and Timing of Leadership

Our vigorous bantering was interspersed with chuckles, giggling, and bursts of laughter. Here we were, the eight members of my Aglow area board sitting around our dining room table discussing an upcoming leadership training session when we ran smack into a good natured impasse over support groups.

"We don't understand them." "We don't want to get involved with this." Then, as if lightning suddenly illuminated their collective idea, they pointed to me with one voice. "Jennie, you do it. You understand them." Their unanimous protests were genial. But I was undaunted.

I looked at my watch and grinned at these wonderful women. "Okay, Ladies," I challenged them. "Push back your chairs. We're going into the living room and 'do' a support group. I'm not going to let you be intimidated by something you haven't experienced."

In spite of their groans, I knew they were with me. Who could miss the honest and loving rapport shining across the faces of this closely knit group?

Not without some apprehension, they settled in to begin

a model support group in the living room. Since one of the women was struggling with fear, I suggested we focus on this issue. We began.

After about twenty minutes I called, "Time's up." My announcement met immediate resistance: "Wait a minute." "We don't want to quit." "This is good." "We're just getting started."

I laughed. "Hey, aren't you the ladies who didn't like support groups?"

Animated, the group plunged into a discussion about what they'd experienced, what they'd learned about themselves, and how they felt about support groups now that they'd had a "taste." To a person, they agreed that leadership was the most essential ingredient of a group. Bev said it adamantly, "I can see that it is imperative to have responsible leadership."

WHAT DOES IT TAKE TO BE A LEADER?

"Are you willing to explore the leadership question in light of our own model?" I posed the question knowing they'd have honest, first-hand reactions. Every head nodded. "Who in the group would you like to have as the leader?" I asked. All eyes riveted on Carol. She was naturally sensitive and yet perceptive in asking challenging questions. "Okay, now," I proceeded, "who would you least like to lead this group?"

"Save your votes, Ladies," giggled Pat. "I know I've been too legalistic. I'm disqualifying myself for leadership. I can't do this. I lack compassion. Listen to me. All I can say is, 'Fear is not of God, so just stop it.'"

"All right, next question," I pursued. "Who *could* lead the group?"

Ginny's hand shot up. "I've got it," she exuded. "I think either one could do it. Carol, the natural, would have less to learn, but even Pat, our legalistic friend, could lead the group if she were called by God and was willing to learn."

This example leads us to our first two essentials of

support group leadership:

First, we must know we have been called by God.

Second, there must be a willingness to yield ourselves to His equipping work and His timing.

GOD'S CALL BRINGS CONFIDENCE

Support group leadership is ministry, clear and simple.

Unless one knows she is called by God to an area of ministry, she is unwise to become involved in it. When we charge ahead on our own, we are moving without God's blessing and provision. For, when He calls us, He also equips us. When we have the assurance of His call, we also have:

- His grace for the task
- His equipping by the Spirit
- His strength for the battle.

When you know that God has called you to a specific ministry, you can serve with full confidence in His provision. This call is also a witness to others, who then can have confidence in God, becoming willing to entrust the delicate areas of their lives to Him through you.

God is very practical. When He gives you His confidence, it is for your protection and the enlargement of His ministry through you. It is no surprise that in every area of ministry, there will be warfare. Satan hates the advancement of God's Kingdom. So if difficulties arise in or around your group, you will feel secure that this is Christ's ministry and that His promise for the Church includes you and your group: "The gates of hell cannot prevail against it."

HOW YOU KNOW GOD'S CALL

I don't know about you, but I've always liked "knowing for sure." This certainly holds true for hearing God's call. Haven't we all, on different occasions, wished at times for a celestial announcement as obvious as the burning bush for Moses or the Damascus Road experience for Paul? If someone just anointed us with oil from our beard to our toes as they did in Old Testament times, we'd know for sure we'd heard from God. Yet most of us will likely know the call of God in much more subtle ways. Let's look at five of these ways:

• *We have an inner knowing.* God impresses His call on our hearts, and our spirit senses it.

• *God often speaks through His Word.* This may be a word confirming something we're already considering or the Holy Spirit making a scripture passage personal to our hearts.

• *God may speak through a prophetic message.* Here again this would most likely be a confirming word to what is already stirring within us.

• *God often "witnesses" to those around us.* They encourage us as they "see" or "know" that God would like to use us in a particular way.

• *God brings something to us repeatedly and we resist it.* This is often a sign that He is calling us over a specific issue and He wants our attention.

In whatever way God has of speaking to us, ultimately we come to the place where we hear Him. The apostle Paul calls this experience, "His Spirit bearing witness to our spirit." When that happens, we must make the choice to obey.

CHOOSING TO OBEY

At an Aglow conference in San Antonio, Texas, Dee Jepson shared her reaction with us when her husband wanted to run for the U.S. Senate. The whole idea of getting involved in the political arena made her uncomfortable and she was reluctant to encourage it. Reluctant that is, until the Lord spoke to her through the scripture: "This is the good work that I prepared in advance for you to do" (See Ephesians 2:10).

Amazingly, when she spoke those words, the Holy Spirit

also nudged me, confirming a decision I needed to make. My term on the Aglow board was up and I didn't know if I was to remain in Aglow leadership. Having this assurance of God's call strengthened me to be obedient to God. Since then, I have been privileged to see hundreds of women changed for eternity through this healing ministry as I've become the U.S. support group resource person.

If I had not recognized the call, I would have missed the glory of God's purpose for my life at this time. Just the thought causes me to tremble. God forbid that we stand before Him one day and see those "good works" He prepared for us to do on one side, and those we chose to do on the other.

By the same token, God forbid that we plunge ahead and attempt to do something for Him when He hasn't called us. Voices other than His can be powerfully enticing, causing us to please people or become a rescuer because "somebody has to." Any motivation other than God's call will not produce fruit for God's Kingdom.

TIMING IS CRUCIAL

The Bible is filled with stories of those whom God called to serve. But in many instances the call and the service were seldom an immediate chain of responses. Most often God required times of maturing and preparation for His servants.

Let's take Samuel in the Old Testament. After his calling by God but before he became a "practicing prophet," scripture says, "Samuel grew and the Lord was with him" (1 Sam. 3:18). Let's take David, anointed when just a shepherd boy. Yet, he learned the ways of God while hiding in caves to save his life before he ascended to his calling as king of Israel.

In the New Testament we are reminded that Paul had several years of learning in Arabia after his conversion and before his active ministry. Even the disciples did not go immediately out on the mission field without Jesus. They served in a three-year process of discipleship training before Pentecost and their full release into the power of the Holy Spirit.

CONSIDER THE TIME ELEMENT

Two additional significant factors fit into our consideration of timing. The first is how much actual time: hours, days, weeks we have to give. We need to ask ourselves if it is possible to do this job given our other responsibilities. Second, is this the right time, considering our obligations, husband, children, job, or other activities?

Bear in mind that women coming to support group are often in tender places in their lives. Being vulnerable and open in itself is risky business and they can be easily wounded if they can't count on your being there for them and being well-prepared. Hurting people—which is almost everyone in the support group—must be able to trust their leaders to fulfill their commitment to the group and thus to them.

Often we can have a call and a sincere desire to become involved in an area of ministry but the obligations to our family and the actual hours we can give simply preclude our saying "yes" to serving at that time. There are times when we need to wait and allow God's plan to unfold more fully.

WORKING ON THE RESPONSIBLE STAGE

God's call, I believe, leads either to a door of service or a door of preparation. In a previous chapter, as you recall, we discussed the three stages of change in your group: becoming aware, becoming responsible, and becoming free. If you are going to lead a support group at a time when you, personally, are in these stages of change, first you will need to determine whether you are at a door of service or a door of preparation.

Suppose, for instance, that you are interested in leading a support group in an area where you have been wounded. Perhaps it was in a divorce. If this is the case, then you will need to work on the *responsible* stage in your own life before you can lead others. If you have not done this, you will probably transfer your own woundedness, usually in the form of anger, bitterness, resentment, hostility, or even deceptive advice onto the women attending the group.

You would never deliberately cause damage or deception. But if you are unhealed, your heart will transfer a wounded message.

KNOWLEDGE MUST BE APPLIED

Often we mistakenly think that knowledge is recovery, that if we know a lot about our area of hurt, we'll be free. However, that is not the case. Women recovering from various issues—abuse, codependence, divorce—may be well informed on the subject, yet remain unhealed. They may still be dealing with anger, performance, rescuing, or other forms of codependency, and it is at these places where they are knowledgeable but unhealed that they will cease helping others and begin using the group to meet their own need or to vent their feelings. When this happens, the group will become unhealthy and the ministry possibly discredited.

I am reminded of Joyce, one of my counseling clients, who was strongly codependent.* She had seen two other counselors prior to coming to me and had read many books on the subject. When she began seeing me, she soon referred two of her friends as well. As I worked separately with her friends, I noted that each applied the information and counsel they received and soon experienced great change in their lives. Seeing their change, Joyce asked me an obvious question: "Why am I still so codependent when I've had all this help?"

She looked at me, puzzled over the gap between her

---

* Codependency is an umbrella term that was first coined to describe the characteristic problems of the spouse of an alcoholic, but has now been broadened to include the issues of people who have centered their lives around rescuing, taking care of, or controlling other people or situations.

friends' progress and hers. I had to give her a hard answer: "You have acquired much knowledge, but you are resistant to change. Often we want our circumstances to change but we don't want to have to be the one to change."

This dear lady heard what I said but was unwilling to go through the pain that change involves. Within a short time, she chose to quit her counseling sessions entirely.

At one time this woman had talked about leading a support group because she was always sharing her information with others. Do I believe she could effectively lead a group?

No. Knowledge alone did not qualify her. In fact, the lack of observable fruit in her life disqualified her.

TAKING RESPONSIBILITY TO CHANGE

A leader must at least be in the *responsible* stage to be of help to others. Here, she is actively applying to her own life the knowledge that she acquired in the *aware* stage. She is clearly taking responsibility to change as well as being open to input from others who may see what she does not. The leader in the responsible stage is actively pursuing restoration in her own life with no pretense of having arrived yet. Being in the responsible stage means that you are open to having others speak truth into your life.

A Christian leader who considered herself healed from the effects of her divorce from an abusive, alcoholic husband was not open for others' input. As a result, many women who sought her help took on very negative attitudes toward men in general. Consequently, their lives and/or marriages became more troubled.

While I believe this precious Christian woman has been greatly used by God, her ministry in this area was premature. God desires to heal and strengthen her, then release her to strengthen other women. We see this principle in action as Christ spoke to Simon Peter: "When you have returned to Me, strengthen your brethren" (Luke 22:32).

PROFILE OF A RESTORED LEADER

Remember, a support group leader will not be perfect, but she has come to a healthy place of wholeness in her life. Let's look briefly at a profile of someone who would be well prepared for leadership.

First, a leader in restoration should no longer be living out of "victim" feelings that can be transferred to others. A restored leader can be discerned by a softness and quietness in her own soul. She is no longer "at war" with her past and can understand God's heart of redemption toward those who have victimized her. Yet, she is a warrior woman who is strong in her resistance to Satan, with a desire to see other captives set free. She is a woman of prayer.

LEADERSHIP REQUIRES PREPARATION

Please note that it is not necessary or required that the group leader have personal experience with the issue the group is confronting. The leader of a group dealing with sexual abuse need not be a sexual abuse victim. The leader of a codependency group need not be a codependent.

When the group leader doesn't bring personal experience to the group, however, she will need to study the issue and become as knowledgeable as possible in order to have compassion and understanding for the experiences of others in the group. She will need to prepare herself adequately enough that the group members feel she truly understands them. This may involve reading several resource materials as well as having contact or interaction with women who have experienced this issue.

If God calls you to lead a group for which you have no personal experience, you can expect Him to give you a sensitivity for those with this problem. You will probably be aware of caring deeply about this issue, feeling real concern and interest in the subject area even before you are called to lead the group.

Even leaders with personal experience will need to

prepare themselves to understand others by reading resource materials and interacting with others of the same or similar experiences.

No one support book can adequately prepare you to lead a group.

I strongly recommend that you study several works on the subject. This will give you a broader scope of the subject and more in-depth understanding which is crucial since no two people in a group will have had exactly the same experience.

In preparing to lead a support group, we would do well to recall Paul's instruction to Timothy: "Do your best to present yourself to God as one approved, a workman who does not need to be ashamed and who correctly handles the word of truth" (2 Tim. 2:15 NIV).

BEING FAITHFUL

When we respond to God's call, He does expect us to be faithful. He knows our lives better than we do and thus will give us His wisdom as to the timing. He desires that we accurately discern His call and His time. Yet this discernment does not always come easily. Some never feel prepared enough and would delay serving while others feel they are ready when they are not.

In the next chapter, we will look at the Aglow leadership requirements which will help you further discern your call and its timing.

6

...

Aglow Leadership Requirements

Years ago, red tape was used to tie up bundles of official U.S. government documents. From this usage, the term became synonymous with doing complicated, frustrating paper procedures.

We usually have a negative picture of red tape: a nightmare of being caught in an escapable paper maze. With pencil in hand we search for a way out, only to find one form after another impeding our progress. Or, if not a maze, we might identify the process with a kitten who bats at a piece of yarn and shortly finds herself hopelessly entangled by the whole ball.

For those of us, such as leaders in Aglow, who occasionally have to deal with paperwork, there is a positive side.

As a brand new recording secretary for my Aglow area board in 1980, one of my first responsibilities was to kindle some excitement (and some follow-through) on having the local officers complete their forms and minutes of their meetings.

However, when I introduced the topic of filling out

leadership forms, no one gave me applause or warm hugs. Instead I heard, "No! Not more forms to fill out. Paper work isn't spiritual. We want to be involved in ministry."

I felt undone. God would have to help me sort this one out. And He did. He brought to mind the book of Numbers.

GOD GIVES US A SENSE OF ORDER

Numbers, the fourth book of the Pentateuch, is one I've often skimmed quickly. After all, those lists didn't seem very meaningful. But in this instance God used this book to show me some very practical things about His ways.

As I read about Israel, I suddenly realized that God didn't need the census, but He knew that the people did. They needed to know who they were, who was with them, what they possessed, and what their capabilities were. When they did their "paperwork" (i.e. the census), Moses and the Israelites gained wisdom for what lay ahead. The census laid the groundwork for the army of the Lord to be formed and the priesthood to be assigned. God was strategically assigning His men for battle and service. He's still doing this with leadership today.

There were other insights from Numbers. I could not miss seeing how God's specific instructions were totally practical for the wilderness journey of His people. His ordinances would bring unity among them and instill dependence on the Lord as they constructed the Tabernacle and moved in to possess the Promised Land. This order enabled Israel to fulfill the purposes of God.

In Numbers 17, I saw another practical parallel for asking leaders to fill out leadership questionnaires. Here God confirms His calling upon Aaron by causing His rod to bud and bring forth life. Aaron's rod was evidence of a complete cycle from barrenness to fruitfulness.

As leaders submit their leadership questionnaires to Aglow in order to lead support groups, those whose call and timing are correct, in a sense, "bud and bear almonds." Everything just comes together and is evidenced to those reviewing the form. The blossoming rod was confirmation to all Israel of God's call upon Aaron's life.

So it is in our ministry. God establishes an order that confirms leadership and enables us to fulfill His purpose.

SUPPORT GROUP LEADERSHIP REQUIREMENTS

Our desire is to make the process of gaining a Certificate of Completion as an Aglow support group leader beneficial to you, yet as uncomplicated as possible. Here are the two steps to follow:

The qualifications for serving as an Aglow support group leader are

1. Submit a leadership questionnaire for approval by your board. If you are already an Aglow leader and have completed a questionnaire in the past, you'll need to complete another, filling in the section specifically for support group leaders. This section consists of three questions which are explained in detail on the following pages.

The following general leadership qualifications are located in section 8, p. 134 of the *Aglow Leader's Digest*:

- You are a born-again believer in Jesus.
- You are baptized in the Holy Spirit, with the evidence of speaking in tongues.
- You are in agreement with Aglow's statement of "What We Believe."
- You hold active membership in Aglow.
- You are a mature Christian, well-grounded in the Word, with a desire to keep growing.
- You can minister in the gifts of the Holy Spirit.

2. Once your board approves your Aglow leadership questionnaire, you may qualify for the support group Certificate of Completion by reading and understanding the biblical truths presented in this book, completing the worksheets located at the back of this book, and sending

them for evaluation to me at the address given on page 202.

Please mail your worksheets as you finish each section of the book, rather than sending them all together. With each worksheet mailed, please enclose a business size (#10), stamped, self- addressed envelope for the reply.

Note! Your worksheets won't be scored or graded, but they will be evaluated to see your grasp of the material and to help guide you in integrating and applying the concepts of support group leadership.

Upon successful completion of the worksheets, you will receive our Certificate of Completion, allowing you to function as an Aglow support group leader.

If for some reason a completion certificate can't be given at the time, you'll receive an explanatory letter.

OUR RESPONSIBILITY IN TOUCHING LIVES

As support group leaders, we touch lives in a deeply personal way. We need both the compassion and the skills to offer the Lord's grace to women wounded by life. Completing the worksheets will help ground you in a basic understanding of Aglow support groups and help establish credibility and accountability for you as a support group leader in this area of Aglow ministry.

Your Certificate of Completion will help give confidence to four key groups of people:

1. Your local or area board, in approving you as a support group leader.

2. The women attending your group; they will know that you have learned biblical truths, and techniques and skills to help them.

3. Those who refer women to an Aglow support group; they will trust your credibility.

4. You; you will know that you have "studied to show yourself approved" and are prepared to lead.

RECOMMENDED READING LIST PROVIDED

A recommended reading list has been provided at the back of this book. When you know what issue your support group will focus on, by all means do the additional reading on that subject to help you better understand the issue and the women in your group. The list certainly is not all-inclusive; it's a starting place for learning more about the issues that most interest you and/or your group.

SPECIFIC SUPPORT GROUP QUESTIONS IN LEADERSHIP QUESTIONNAIRE

Under the section, Support Group Leadership, in Aglow's leadership questionnaire, you'll find three questions.

1. What is the topic of the support group you will be leading?

2. In what ways do you feel qualified to facilitate/lead this support group?

3. Are you willing to work toward developing your support group skills by attending training seminars as scheduled?

These are basic questions, but they will help your board discern your willingness and your readiness to serve. Let's see what the board will be looking for in your answers.

For question #1, they'll look to see if the leader is interested in an issue she has experienced personally. If so, they will want to know that she has come into responsibility regarding this issue in her own life, as we discussed in the previous chapter. For example, they would not approve a woman who wanted to lead a group on grief if she was still venting anger at God for "allowing her son to die."

For question #2, they would need to know that a woman with or without personal experience was open to training. If she has had experience in groups other than Aglow, they would need to know that she is willing to use the Aglow format and guidelines. Here a word of explanation will help: Often we have Aglow women who have received help from other groups and they want Aglow to do it "that way" because they've experienced real healing from that group. But we at Aglow feel a definite call to what we have established and believe we need to be consistent in offering ministry in the distinct ways God has shown us.

This doesn't mean we are inflexible. We are very open to your suggestions, but our guidelines should be followed until changes are incorporated ministry-wide or until you are given permission to adapt your suggestions. We are not in competition with other groups; we regard and respect their ways and results. But we must be true to our own distinct ministry, and we desire that this particular expression be consistent throughout the Aglow support network. (See pp. 140-145 for more detail.)

Question #3 is easy to understand, but the answer is so important, it needs considering. All leaders must be teachable, eager to grow, and open to change and personal growth, desiring to be as prepared for their area of ministry as possible. A woman, for instance, who does not have time for training is probably too busy to lead effectively. (See Chapter Five, page 58, under subhead, "Consider the Time Element").

A woman who feels she needs no additional training may have a pride problem that could interfere with her being an effective leader. Please note that Aglow is not applying legalistic conditions here; we recognize that circumstances can prevent a leader from attending occasionally. What we are looking for is the attitude and willingness of the leader's heart.

EVALUATING YOURSELF AS A GROUP LEADER

There are also nine personal leadership qualifications it may be helpful for you to consider. A support group leader needs to be reacting towards and maturing in these areas as she seeks to lead. I suggest that you evaluate yourself in the following nine areas by using this system:

Place a *1* if you have no experience with this.

Place a *2* if you are consciously working at this.

Place a *3* if you feel competent with this.

Your numbers will help you focus on the areas you need to work on as you begin leading your group. From time to time go back and look at your evaluation and see if your numbers are changing. You might even want to have a friend go over it with you and give her input as to how she sees you growing in these areas.

1. *Courage*: As you consider courage, first read 1 Corinthians 16:13-14. Then look at the ways a leader shows courage:

_____ She is open to self-disclosure, admitting her own mistakes and taking the same risks she expects others to take.

_____ She lovingly explores areas of struggle with women, and looks beyond their behavior to hear what's in their hearts.

_____ She is secure in her own beliefs, sensitive to the Holy Spirit's prompting, and willing to act upon them.

_____ She draws on her own experiences to help her identify with others in the group and be emotionally touched by them.

_____ She continually examines her own life in the light of God's Word and the Holy Spirit's prompting.

_____ She is direct and honest with members, not using her role to protect herself from interaction with the group.

_____ She knows that wholeness is the goal and that change is a process.

2. *Willingness to Model*: As you consider willingness to model, read Psalm 139:23-24. Then look at the ways a

leader shows a willingness to lead in the following ways:

_____ She should have had some moderate victory in her own struggles, with adequate healing having taken place. If she is not whole in the area she is leading, she should at least be fully aware of her unhealed areas and not be defensive of them. She should be open to those who can show her if she is misguiding others by ministering out of her own hurt.

_____ She understands that a group leader leads largely by example, by doing what she expects members to do.

_____ She is no longer "at war" with her past and can be compassionate to those who may have victimized her. Yet she is a "warrior woman," strong in her resistance to Satan, with a desire to see other captives set free.

3. *Presence*: Read Galatians 6:2 as you consider *presence*. A leader shows her *presence* with the group in the following ways:

_____ She needs to either have had personal experience with a support group or observed enough so she understands how it functions.

_____ She needs to be in touch with her own feelings so that she can have compassion for and empathy with other women.

_____ She must understand that her role is as facilitator. She is not to be the answer person, for she is not responsible for change in others. Yet she must be able to evidence leadership qualities that enable her to gather a group around her.

4. *Goodwill and Caring*: As you consider goodwill and caring, read Matthew 22:27-28. Now look at the ways a leader shows these qualities:

_____ She needs to express genuine caring, even for

those who are not easy to care for. This takes a commitment to love and a sensitivity to the Holy Spirit.

_____ She should be able to express caring by (1) inviting women to participate but allowing them to decide how far to go; (2) giving warmth, concern and support when, and only when, it is genuinely felt; (3) gently confronting a participant when there are obvious discrepancies between her words and her behavior; and (4) encouraging people to be who they are without the masks and shields.

_____ She will need to be able to maintain focus in the group.

5. *Openness*: As you consider openness, read Ephesians 4:15-16. A leader shows her openness in the following ways:

_____ She must be aware of herself, open to others in the group, open to new experiences, and open to life styles and values that are different from her own.

_____ She needs to have an attitude of openness, not revealing every aspect of her personal life, but disclosing enough of herself to give participants a sense of who she is.

_____ She needs to recognize her own weaknesses and not spend energy concealing them from others. A strong sense of awareness allows her to be vulnerable with the group.

6. *Nondefensiveness*: As you consider nondefensiveness, read 1 Peter 5:5. A leader shows her nondefensiveness in the following way:

_____ She needs to be secure in her leadership role. When negative feelings are expressed, she must be able to explore them in a nondefensive manner.

7. *Stamina*: As you consider stamina, read Ephesians 6:10. A leader shows her stamina in the following ways:

_____ She needs physical and emotional stamina and the ability to withstand pressure and remain vitalized until the group sessions end.

_____ She must be aware of her own energy level, have outside sources of spiritual and emotional nourishment, and have realistic expectations for the group's progress.

8. *Perspective*: As you consider perspective, read Proverbs 3:5-6. A leader shows her perspective in the following ways:

_____ She needs to cultivate a healthy perspective that allows her to enjoy humor and be comfortable with the release of it at appropriate times in a meeting.

_____ Although she will hear pain and suffering, she must trust the Lord to do the work and not take responsibility for what He alone can do.

_____ She needs to have a good sense of our human condition and God's love, as well as a good sense of timing that allows her to trust the Holy Spirit to work in the women's lives.

9. *Creativity*: As you consider creativity, read Philippians 1:9-11. A leader shows her creativity in the following way:

_____ She needs to be flexible and spontaneous, able to discover fresh ways to approach each session.

I am certain you can see by this time that we must be very responsible with support group leadership. We must compassionately offer these wounded women our Lord's healing grace. To do this, our motives must be pure, our preparation complete, and our lives committed to serving Christ.

7
...

Our Weaknesses and Our Strengths

The purpose of this chapter is to guide us in taking an honest, in-depth look at ourselves.

I like what Lois Burkett, a prominent minister to leaders, says about you and me. She says we are "divine originals." God has indeed created each of us unique human beings, "special orders," designed to live our lives for His eternal purposes. Yet, because we have been born into a sin-filled world and bear sin in our nature, we fall far short of being what God intended.

It follows then that in order to serve God effectively in support group ministry, we must deal truthfully with who we are. We must face the fact that our lives have both weak and strong areas to contend with. Such knowledge, although at times sobering, should inevitably drive us desperately—and eagerly—to yield our lives to the Holy Spirit.

KNOWING WEAKNESSES AND STRENGTHS

An effective leader must know both her weaknesses and her strengths. Why is such self-knowledge so crucial? Let me answer with three examples, the first two from the

Bible and the second from my own life.

In the book of Judges we read that God calls Gideon to go forth boldly in battle against the Midianites. Such a venture terrifies Gideon: his immediate response is to protest the assignment. "But Lord, how can I save Israel? My clan is the weakest in Manasseh, and I am the least in my family" (Judges 6:15).

Gideon is scared, and he makes no pretense of his insecurity as he enumerates his weaknesses to the Lord. But the Lord is not put off by Gideon's fear. There is no rebuke; instead God urges him on with the assurance that He Himself will cover for his deficiencies:

> Go in the strength you have and save Israel. . . . Am I not sending you? . . . I will be with you, and you will strike down all the Midianites together (Judges 6:14, 16 NIV).

We see a similar example in the story of David and Goliath. Young David knew he was no match for the powerful Philistine giant. He was far too weak and inexperienced even to make a showing against such strength, unless . . . unless he came against him "in the name of the Lord Almighty, the God of the armies of Israel" (See 1 Samuel 17:45). This is precisely what David did. Relying on God's strength he killed his enemy, Goliath, whose only strength lay in his own flesh.

These two instances clearly indicate that we don't need knowledge of our strengths and weaknesses for its own sake. We need it so we can call on God to be strong in the face of our weakness and to give us grace in the face of our strength.

A PERSONAL EXAMPLE

As a Christian, I must accept the fact that I have two natures and that these natures do not complement each other. I have an "old man" or human nature that Scripture encourages me to "take off" and I have a "new" nature in

Christ Jesus that I am to be "putting on."

In the story of Gideon, his first response to God was from his human nature, and his self-consciousness and inadequacies responded to God. David responded from the nature of God within him. I find that I do both. Sometimes I respond to life from my human nature and at other times I respond from my Christ nature. When I respond from my human nature, I am challenged by the Christ in me to change; much as Gideon was.

But in order to change natures, I must recognize my human nature and differentiate it from my Christ nature. This takes honesty. I must honestly take a look at myself and objectively assess my behaviors, thoughts, and feelings. As I have done this, let me share with you what I see in myself.

First, the good things: I like people and am friendly. I smile easily and this helps others feel accepted. I am gentle. I have a loud side but I also have a quiet side. I am optimistic and enjoy new things and expect the best. I may be hurt because of fear of rejection, but I forgive and actually forget easily.

I lead naturally but I like working with others. I like being part of a team. I have vision and commitment.

Now for the more difficult parts I see in me: I may want to tell you what to do and perhaps be controlling as well. I will want to have fun and not be too serious. I may talk about myself too much, and I may not be disciplined enough to help you to the goal I have said you must reach. I have some insecurity and may withdraw from authority figures. At times I over-obligate myself and put myself under time pressure.

For six years I have been counseling on a daily basis, and I can tell those times when my "natural self" is too present and I am too directive or too light-hearted. Most often at these times the Holy Spirit convicts me so I can take responsibility to change. In Christ I can be others-centered, disciplined, and non-controlling.

My motivational gifts (from Romans 12:6-8) are exhortation, teaching, and prophecy. All these gifts are good gifts for a counselor because through them I see where you want to be and I know how to get you there. And what is more, I believe you can make it!

However, because they are what I call "mouth" gifts, when joined to the weaknesses of my self-nature, I will be inclined to talk too much when a counselor's job is to listen. As you can see, even these God given gifts must be submitted to the Christ in me.

A LOOK IN THE MIRROR

Take out a sheet of paper and do what I did. Take a look at yourself. Go ahead. No one is looking and no one will know but you. You need to know yourself.

You may have heard of counselors asking people to list ten things they like about themselves in order to work on their self-esteem. Many people have trouble looking at themselves. But as leaders, if we do not know ourselves, we will be hindered in effectively helping others.

Once I played a game in a church home group where they passed around a roll of toilet tissue and you were to tear off as much as you wanted. Then they told us that for each square of tissue you took, you had to tell something good about yourself. I liked that game. But it really challenged some of the people. Some cried, even though it was good to take a look at ourselves. Now, make these three lists on your paper:

1. Positive parts of myself
2. Difficult parts of myself
3. How do I see these positive/difficult parts affecting me as I lead a support group?

After you have your list, you would benefit from sharing it with a close friend. Ask her if she agrees with what you see in yourself. Ask if she would add anything. Consider her feedback as you desire to honestly see yourself.

As you take a look at your strengths and weaknesses, you can also see how they can conflict. For example, I like people and want them to like me, but when I'm bossy, no one wants to be around me. My weakness cancels out my strength. Or my own strength can interfere. If I am laid back and easygoing, that is nice. But if I procrastinate as I take it easy, then I'm actually creating stress. If I'm a careful thinker, that is good. But if I'm overanalytical and never make decisions then that is a problem. If I like a sense of order, that is helpful. But if I demand perfection, then I'll never be happy.

FOCUSING ON THE FRUITS

Seeing ourselves clearly is good, but what are we to do with these areas of conflict? The answer has been given by the Lord through the Apostle Paul in Galatians 5:22-23:

> The fruit of the Spirit is love, joy, peace, longsuffering, kindness, goodness, faithfulness, gentleness, self-control.

One of the marks of a maturing Christian is the evidence of the fruits of the Spirit in her life. This is our Christ nature. When we honestly see our strengths and weaknesses, then we can yield them to this nature of Christ within us. His nature enhances our strengths and overcomes our weaknesses.

Is there anything more enticing, more pleasant than the aroma of a fruitful vine of fragrant grapes hanging in mouth-watering clusters, or crisp red apples wafting their freshness across the orchard? When we see such delectable fruits in their stunning fullness, we know we are beholding something very good.

The same holds true for the fruits of the Spirit. They are irresistible. When we see them in someone's life, we sense nothing short of the loving presence of the Lord Jesus.

Let's take a close look at the fruits of the Spirit, at this harvest straight from the heart of a loving God:

Love
: A supernatural love that causes us to love God and others more than ourselves
A love that causes us to love our enemies
A love that causes us to love the Kingdom of God more than the material world and our own life

Joy
: An expression from within apart from our circumstances
A result of our life focusing on Christ, rather than on people or problems
The opposite of depression, doubt, dejection, dreariness, and despair

Peace
: The "peace of God" that is imparted from Him
"Peace with God" which is from right-standing relationship with Him

Longsuffering
: Patience, endurance, dependability
Work that endures with a right attitude

Kindness
: Tenderness. A heart that is thoughtful, polite, gracious, considerate, understanding when under pressure as well as in easy times

Goodness
: Seeks the good of and for others before and instead of self

Faithfulness
: A complete abandonment of yourself to God

	An absolute dependence upon God for yourself Frees you to "be" for others Absence of fear
Meekness	Humble, mild, submissive, yielding Non-asserting of self
Self-control	Self-discipline, submitted to control of Holy Spirit Consistent, dependable, well-ordered, steady, steadfast

The Holy Spirit works in us to produce the fruits of the Spirit. As we cooperate with Him, in honest repentance and loving obedience, the weaknesses of our human nature are transformed.

The part of my human nature that wants to control is not meek. Through prayer, however, I can submit this weakness to God and choose to be meek in Christ. I can choose these fruits rather than my old nature.

Look at the lists you did. With what fruits can you choose to replace your weaknesses?

The fruits of the Spirit transform our human nature into the nature of Christ.

And how about the women in your support group? The gospel message shouts that such transformation can be a reality. Jesus paid the price for that "old" part of us, our sin nature, that we might put on His "new" nature.

Paul says it so well in his letter to the Ephesians:

You were taught with regard to your former way of life, to put off your old self, which is being corrupted by its deceitful desires; to be made new in the attitude of your minds; and to put on the new self, created to be like God in true righteousness and holiness (Eph. 4:22-23 NIV).

8

...

Looking at Your Gifts

Say, "gifts" and we all come running. It's not just four-year-old children who dance on one foot at their birthday parties, pleading with their mothers to "start opening presents NOW."

Most of us would admit that the little kid inside all of us still dances at the thought of unwrapping a gift. Sure, we sophisticated adults may cover up our feelings a bit when someone hands us a gorgeous package and says, "This is for you." But inside, our heart is doing cartwheels as we rip off the ribbons and tear through the paper. Someone has risked making an investment in us.

Gifts send a message that we're special, valuable, even lovable. According to God's own Word, we are all of the above. We are so beloved, in fact, that the Creator of the universe has showered us, not only with life itself, but with "designer gifts" especially fashioned for us to use for the strengthening of His entire family.

In this chapter we will be looking at gifts the Lord has given us: motivational gifts, gifts for ministry, and even the gift of life's experiences.

First, let's look at the motivational gifts.

MOTIVATIONAL GIFTS

As support group leaders we need an understanding of what motivates us to minister or care for others. The Apostle Paul explains in Romans 12:5-8 that by God's grace we have each been given gifts that move us to minister to other members of the Body of Christ.

> In Christ we who are many form one body, and each member belongs to all the others. We have different gifts, according to the grace given us. If a man's gift is prophesying, let him use it in proportion to his faith. If it is serving, let him serve; if it is teaching, let him teach; if it is encouraging, let him encourage; if it is contributing to the needs of others, let him give generously; if it is leadership, let him govern diligently; if it is showing mercy, let him do it cheerfully (NIV).

These motivational gifts move us to reach out in a particular way. As an encourager and teacher I am moved to give you the instruction in this book so you can be a great support group leader.

Let's look at a description of each gift:

Prophesying	This gift is concerned with establishing and fulfilling God's plans
Serving	This gift is concerned with meeting the needs of others in practical ways that facilitate the work of God taking place
Teaching	This gift is concerned with imparting the truth and knowledge of God's Word
Exhorting	This gift is concerned with encouraging spiritual development
Giving	This gift is concerned with providing the financial and functional means so

	ministry can be accomplished
Leadership	This gift is concerned with administrating and keeping order to facilitate ministry
Mercy	This gift is concerned with the emotional needs of the Body of Christ

If four of us sat down to discuss how to begin a support group, we would have different approaches because our gifts would move us differently. For instance:

(Helen) "I want to make sure everyone has a book and that the room is arranged comfortably." What gift is this?

_____

(Sue) "I want everyone to be glad they came. I will start with an ice-breaker so everyone can relax." What gift is this?

_____

(Linda) "I want to share the vision and purpose for our group." What gift is this?

_____

(Karen) "I want to start by sharing my story so everyone knows I understand how they feel and will be comfortable sharing their story." What gift is this?

_____

Which approach is best? It depends on you. No one approach is better. It is just different. Each woman is motivated by her own perspective about what is important. All of their ideas need to be put into action, and our motivational gift will determine what approach we will take first or what we will think of first.

What would be your approach?

_____

_____

_____

As we mature in Christ, we manifest all of the gifts to some extent. A friend shared with me that when she first got saved she thought very little about giving but now it is very important to her. Yet her first response in a situation is to get things organized. What gift is this?

Look over the scriptures in Romans and ask the Lord to reveal to you what your gifts are.

What moves you first in a situation?

_____

_____

_____

_____

As I mentioned in the previous chapter, my gifts are the "mouth" gifts. This can be a problem if I don't stop to listen to others or, as I have sometimes found, I can get so absorbed in teaching that I don't notice that people have quit listening. All gifts can be overdone. We must keep the use of our God-given gifts submitted to the Holy Spirit.

A server can overdo it by never allowing others to do for themselves or by wearing herself out and feeling like a martyr ("I'm the only one who ever arranges the chairs").

A leader/administrator can forget to relate personally because she is busy taking care of details.

A prophet may become depressed because people are not grasping the truth and changing more quickly.

The mercy person may be afraid to allow people to hurt or may carry too many burdens for others and become emotionally drained.

Think about your gifts. How will they help you as a support group leader? Do you see any potential problems?

God is so gracious that as He has called the Body of Christ to minister one to another, He has equipped each of us with the precise gifts that enable us.

MINISTRY GIFTS

When I think of ministry gifts, I think of my friend on the West Coast who loves giving homemade food gifts for Christmas. She insists she's twice blessed. As she stands at her stove, stirring her wild blackberry jelly, she savors every turn of the wooden spoon in her hand, every whiff of the bubbling berries.

The process reminds her of that sun-drenched July day when she and her daughter found the hidden berry patch and plucked the prizes for her freezer. A blessing of a day.

But now, in cold December, the blessing of the precious wild berries continues. In fact, it doubles. My friend gives the jelly away to her family and friends and they—and their muffins and toast—are blessed. Her heart is satisfied, and once again she is blessed.

There is a parallel in the blessing God has for you, and for His Body, in ministering the manifestation gifts of the Holy Spirit. These gifts that we minister to one another in the Body of Christ are found in 1 Corinthians 12:7-10.

- Word of Wisdom—Godly wisdom showing us what to do
- Word of Knowledge—Information imparted super-naturally
- Faith—Faith that transcends our own human faith
- Gifts of Healing—Various manifestations of healing

- Working of Miracles—Intervention in the natural order
- Prophecy—Speaking out the revelation of God
- Discerning of Spirits—Ability to know what spirit is at work
- Tongues—A divinely imparted prayer language, used with interpretation, to edify the Body of Christ
- Interpretation of Tongues—Divine interpretation of a tongue

One of the basic leadership requirements of Aglow is the ability to minister these gifts from the Holy Spirit to others. As we are open and available to the Holy Spirit, He ministers them through our lives to those in need.

YOUR ROLE IN MINISTERING THESE GIFTS

As a support group leader you need to be familiar with these gifts and open for them to work through you. You will use them at the end of group meetings when women seek prayer. Also, as the leader, you will more than likely receive them during the group time. The Lord will likely use these gifts—words of knowledge, wisdom, discerning of spirits, etc., to give you His insight into a specific situation or what individual women may be needing. The Holy Spirit wants to be a "very present helper" in your group.

I encourage you to pray before your group meeting. Ask the Lord for a fresh in-filling of the Holy Spirit and tell Him you desire His ministry to be available through you. If you feel you need a specific gift, such as words of wisdom for your group, then pray specifically for that gift to be manifested.

I often tell leaders, you will "lead with two ears"; your natural ear will be open to hear the women and your spiritual ear will be open to the voice of the Holy Spirit.

It is the anointing of the Holy Spirit that will bypass your human ability and touch the women at their precise point of need. Let His Spirit bring liberty through your life.

THE GIFT OF LIFE EXPERIENCE

Have you ever thought of life experience as a gift? In a very real way, it is.

Think of it this way: you bring to your support group a special, individual experience of life. As you are "unwrapped" before them, the women receive who and what you have become through your experience of living. It is an enriching gift to them. They, in turn, will also receive this gift from one another in the group.

Perhaps you can see already that this last section is very personal, and it needs to be; support group ministry is very personal. The paradox is that we are all so much the same yet so distinctly different. You will find in your groups that it will be a common wound or other experience that brings women to your group; they will, in many ways, have the same feelings and thoughts. Yet, no two lives are exactly the same.

We are all very much individual. Your life experiences are individually yours. No two children born to the same parents experience the same parents in the same way. The age of the parents and life situations at the time each child was born and raised changes. Even the way the parents' and child's temperaments interact will be different in each case.

In the same way, your life experience will affect the way you respond to the women in your group—the way you lead the group. We have said that it is not necessary to personally experience the issue the group is dealing with, but not experiencing the issue will affect your perspective and you must be aware of this.

BITTER OR BETTER?

Someone has said that life either makes us bitter or better. Think back on your experiences.

Are you better? If there are areas you are not sure about, you will need to be aware of these "hard" places where you may have become bitter. This will inevitably show itself to the group.

Life experiences also have the wonderful effect of accelerating maturity. When we have matured through life experience we are often much more "fruity." Faithfulness, long-suffering, gentleness, kindness—the fruits of the Spirit are usually much more evident in our lives.

Remember, too, that age is not the determining factor for maturity. We can be advanced in age but our response to life experiences may hinder our maturity. Likewise, we can be young in years, yet matured through what life has brought us. We can count on the fact that the more we have been matured by life experiences the more understanding we will be with the process of change in our group.

Our all-knowing Lord foresees that life is difficult and has provided through His Son and His Holy Spirit healing, comfort, compassion, and strength. He desires that we comfort with the same comfort we have received, having freely received, freely give.

A FINAL WORD . . . YOUR ESSENCE

It is our desire that you have learned much about yourself by now and have been challenged to keep growing. You now see many things that will affect you as you lead your group. The purpose of this section, "To Know Yourself," is to help you know who you are.

There is just one more very important thing: It is like the bouquet of flowers that, when put in place, makes the table setting perfect.

This special part of you is your *essence. Essence* is defined as "that which makes a thing what it is." Ask yourself this question: "What makes me what I am?"

Your essence is that you are the object of divine affection. The words from 1 John say it so well:

This is how God showed his love among us: He sent his one and only Son into the world that we might live through him. This is love: not that we loved God, but that he loved us and sent his Son as an atoning sacrifice for our sins. Dear friends, since God so loved us, we also ought to love one another" (1 John 4:9-11 NIV).

Hurting people often ask, "Why was I born?" "What is my life for anyway?" "What does God want with me?" The answer for all of these questions is essence: we are the objects of His love. He has set His love upon us through Christ Jesus.

God has chosen us as His very own. Living in the reality of our true essence as God sees us transforms us, frees us. The more fully we receive our essence and live out of it, the more free we are to be His fragrance of life to others.

The following material adapted from a teaching by Mary Lance Sisk, a member of the Aglow International Board, will help you embrace your essence in the light of our Father's love.

Mary says, "The number one tactic of the enemy (flesh, world, and the devil) is to distort the character of God so you will live in constant fear and unbelief. Our natural parents do not always manifest God's character to us; therefore, our concept of God can be distorted from our earliest childhood memories. It is vital to learn God's character and His ways as revealed through His Word."[1]

MY HEAVENLY FATHER IS A GRACIOUS LOVING PARENT

1. He is love. John 3:16; 1 John 4:8-10, 16
2. He loves me with an everlasting love. Jer. 31:3
3. He loves me with the same intensity He loves His Son, Jesus. John 17:23; Eph. 2:4
4. He will not let anything separate me from His love. Rom. 8:35-39
5. He chose me from the foundation of the world and totally and unconditionally accepts me in the Beloved. Eph. 1:4-6
6. I am His beloved child and I can call Him Father. Rom. 8:15; Gal. 4:4-6
7. He will carry me all the days of my life just as a man carries his child. Deut. 1:31; Isa. 46:3, 4
8. He cherishes and honors me. Isa. 43:4
9. I am precious in His sight. Isa. 43:4
10. I am His own possession, His special treasure. Deut 4:20, 7:6; Ex. 19:5, 6

11. He rejoices over me with singing.* Zeph. 3:17
12. He exults over me with joy.* Zeph. 3:17
13. He takes pleasure in me. Ps. 149:4; Rev. 4:11
14. He meets all of my needs according to His riches in Christ Jesus. Ps. 23:1-6, 36:8; Phil. 4:19; Prov. 3:9, 10, 11:24, 25
15. He bears all of my burdens. Ps. 55:22; 1 Pet. 5:7
16. He gives me rest. Matt. 11:28-30; Heb. 4:9-11; Ps. 23:2
17. He leads me as a gentle shepherd. Ps. 23:1; Isa. 40:11
18. He lavishes me with His grace. Eph. 1:7, 8
19. He crowns me with tender mercies. Ps. 103:4 (KJV); Eph. 2:4, 5
20. He does not remember my sins and iniquities. Heb. 8:12; Ps. 103:10-12
21. He is absolutely trustworthy.* Ps. 9:10, 33:20-22; Prov. 28:25; Isa. 12:2; Jer. 17:5-8; Matt. 12:17-21
22. He will not abandon me . . . ever leave me or forsake me.* Heb. 13:5; Matt. 28:20; Deut. 31:6-8; Josh. 1:5; 1 Sam. 12:22
23. He will not fail me. 1 Chr. 28:20; Ps. 89:33-37; Deut. 4:31
24. He keeps all of His promises to me.* Josh. 21:43-45, 23:14; 1 Kings 8:56; 2 Cor. 1:20; 2 Pet. 1:4
25. He will never lie to me.* Heb. 6:18; Num. 23:19; 1 Sam. 15:29; Titus 1:2
26. He is absolutely stable . . . He never changes.* Mal. 3:6; Jas. 1:17; Heb. 13:8
27. He only wants the highest good for me.* Ps. 31:19, 52:1, 103:5, 107:8, 9; Zech. 9:16, 17; Rom. 2:4; 2 Thess. 1:11
28. He guards me as the apple of His eye. Deut. 32:10; Ps. 17:8
29. He keeps me from evil. Ps. 121, 31:7, 8; John 17:12-15; 2 Thess. 3:3; 1 Pet. 2:25
30. He fights my battles for me and wins all of them. Deut. 1:30, 31; 1 Sam. 17:45-47; Neh. 4:20; 2 Tim. 4:17, 18
31. He executes vengeance for me so I can rest in peace.** Deut. 32:35; Heb. 10:30
32. He will vindicate me.** Deut. 32:36; Ps. 7:8; Isa. 54:13
33. No one can pluck me out of His hands. John 10:27-29
34. He gives me peace and doesn't want me to be anxious or worried about anything.** 1 Cor. 14:33; Gal. 5:22; Phil. 4:7; Col. 3:15; 2 Thess. 3:16
35. He revives me when I am weary and exhausted.** Ps. 68:9, 119:107; Isa. 40:28-31, 57:15; Matt. 11:28-30; Rom. 8:11
36. He disciplines me with love and justice. Prov. 3:11, 12; Heb. 12:6-11; Deut. 32:4; John 5:30
37. He has blessed me with every heavenly gift. Eph. 1:3
38. He has given me an everlasting kingdom and made me His own possession. Dan. 7:18; 1 Pet. 2:9
39. He has given me an inheritance making me a fellow heir with His son, Jesus. Rom. 8:16, 17; Gal. 3:29; Eph. 1:11-14; Col. 1:12-14
40. He has taken away the fear of death. I will never die. Heb. 2:14,15;

John 11:25, 26
41. He has given me a spirit of love, not fear. Rom. 8:15; 2 Tim. 2:7
42. He will present me faultless before His presence with exceeding joy.** 2 Tim. 4:18; Jude 24
43. He is a GRACIOUS LOVING PARENT! Ex. 22:27; Ps. 103:11-14, 111:4; 1 Pet. 2:3 (KJV); Isa. 9:6; 1 Cor. 6:16-18

Amen and amen.

You have now completed the reading in Section Two. Please turn to the worksheets for this section on page 207, and reproduce a copy. Then fill in your answers on the copy. If you are applying to become an Aglow support group leader, mail your completed sheets to Jennie Newbrough at the address on page 202. Be sure to include a stamped, self-addressed, business size (#10) envelope to facilitate their return. If you are reading for your own edification, you also may want to reproduce the worksheets, fill them in, and keep them as part of your self-study.

---

*These truths speak to the wounds many have had by natural fathers or other men.
** Victims particularly respond to these truths.

Section III

To Know People

THE PRIVILEGE   of this section is to see within humanity as God sees.

THE CHALLENGE   of this section is to understand internal messages and motives within human beings as God does.

9
...

Longings and Lies

When someone knows us "inside and out" and accepts us as we are, we feel deeply loved and cherished.

That's how God relates to us. In His graciousness, He always remembers our true nature and He loves us with tender compassion. Listen to the psalmist as he pictures this rich truth:

> As a father has compassion on his children, so the Lord has compassion on those who fear him; for he knows how we are formed, he remembers we are dust (Ps. 103:13-14 NIV).

As support group leaders, we also need to have this heart of remembrance and compassion, recognizing that people are in the group because of their desire to change.

In this chapter we will look at some of the basic issues common to mankind, issues that affect the reason women have for coming to a support group and their participation in the group. First we'll begin with looking at our deepest human needs and our most common wound.

OUR DEEPEST NEEDS

Mankind's deepest needs are for love, acceptance, and approval. It is in relationship with the Lord that these needs can be fulfilled. Let's take a closer look at each:

Love   This is love; not that we loved God, but that he loved us and sent his Son as an atoning sacrifice for our sin (1 John 4:10 NIV).

Acceptance   Blessed be the God and Father of our Lord Jesus Christ, who has blessed us with every spiritual blessing in the heavenly places in Christ, just as He chose us in Him before the foundation of the world, that we should be holy and without blame before Him in love, having predestined us to adoption as sons by Jesus Christ to Himself, according to the good pleasure of His will, to the praise of the glory of His grace by which He has made us accepted in the Beloved (Eph. 1:3-6).

Approval   For not he who commends himself is approved, but whom the Lord commends. (2 Cor. 10:18).

Sadly, many people cannot receive love, acceptance, and approval from the Lord, for they have been deeply affected by this common wound of mankind: Rejection.

REJECTION AND THE ULTIMATE LIE

Born with a sin nature inherited from our first parents' disobedience, we "fallen men" reject one another in a multitude of hurtful ways. God, however, never turned away from those He created to love, never rejected them, even when they sinned against Him.

But He did reject Satan. In retaliation for this action against him, Satan attacked—and continues to attack—God's creation, deceiving mankind and perpetuating the lie that we are not loved, accepted, or approved of by others or by God. In the misery of his true rejection, Satan wants us to suffer with him.

The effect of this works out in what I call the pattern of the *ultimate lie*. This pattern has a cycle that Satan exploits to keep us entrapped in sinful behavior.

CYCLE OF THE ULTIMATE LIE

Note the drawing below as an illustration of the painful and destructive pattern that is set in motion when a wound occurs followed by Satan's attack:

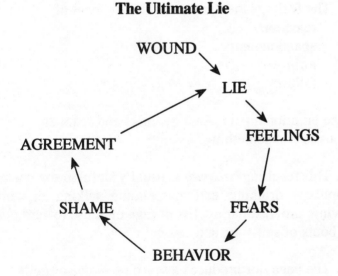

The Ultimate Lie

The following explanation gives clarity to this cycle:

1. A *wound* is an opening through which Satan seeks access to our lives. Then, into each significant wound he imparts a lie.

The lie invariably expresses rejection:
>
> I'm not wanted.
> I'm bad.
> I'm not good enough.
> No one loves me.
> I shouldn't live.

2. The wound may heal with time or be forgotten, but the *lie* remains embedded within our human spirit.

3. The embedded lie produces underlying *feelings* that are similar to the lie:
>
> I'm ugly.
> I'm all alone.
> I can't do anything right.

4. The feelings then produce primary *fears* of
>
> rejection
> abandonment
> intimacy
> failure

The emotional pain of the feelings and fears then compels us to "do something."

5. This resulting *behavior* is usually sinful in some way: compulsive drinking, eating, spending, talking, or withdrawing, procrastinating, fits of rage or abuse toward others, bouts of self-pity, and so on.

6. The behavior produces a sense of *shame* or guilt.

7. Internally we *agree* with the lie:
>
> Why should anyone love me?
> Look at the way I act.
> I'm not worth caring about.
> I'll never be any good.

Now we are just where Satan wants us. We no longer believe God's truth about us. Instead, we are *in agreement* with Satan and his lies, in bondage to his deception, and entrapped in a cycle of sin and rejection.

The wonderful news is that Satan need not have the last word! In His redemptive love, the Lord desires to bring His truth to triumph over this pattern of lies and rejection. The truth of His love, acceptance, and approval can bring liberty to those held captive by the lies of the enemy.

A NEW PATTERN

Satan's lies fall flat when routed by God's truth. Look now at how the pattern of woundedness is altered when this happens:

A New Pattern

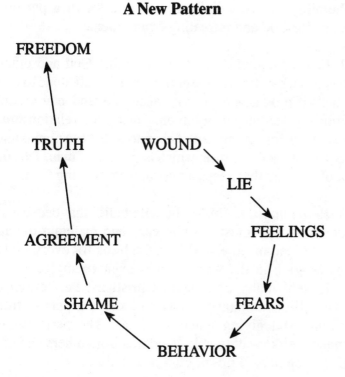

In her book *Adult Children and the Almighty* Melinda Fish expounds on the effect of a wounded soul. She makes a very strong statement: "When the soul is not restored a victim cannot be led by the Spirit, but they are led by a wounded soul."[1]

The Lord wants to bring us to a place where we are no longer led by a wounded soul; He wants to restore our soul. Many who come to your groups will bear wounded souls. In her book, Melinda lists the following eight emotional difficulties that are indications of a wounded soul in a Christian's life:

1. *Low self-esteem*: This is a person's inability to see herself as lovable by God and others, remaining therefore unworthy of redemption and restoration. It masquerades as humility but is actually a major factor in a person's disobeying God and retreating from others.

2. *Fear of abandonment*: The fear that God and others will leave her and that in the end she will be left alone to fend for herself produces hyper-vigilance, the tendency to look continually for danger in circumstances and relationships. Like any other fear, the fear of abandonment can manipulate a person into compromise, which is the fear of man. This the root of all fears that keeps a person from trusting God.

3. *Perfectionism*: This is the core belief that because of imperfection we must work to earn and maintain the approval of God or others. This is the basis for every idolatrous religion in the world and is even entangled in the emotions of many born-again Christians. Perfectionism creates all-or-nothing thinking and keeps a person from receiving and giving grace to others. The perfectionist demands seldom-attainable standards from others and herself, setting herself up for continual failure.

4. *Authority problems*: Rebellion against authority is

the natural outflow of the fearful life, the thought life of the person who deeply believes that God does not have her best interest at heart and cannot, therefore, protect her from others who will take advantage of her. Unless the person is healed, she cannot become an integral, productive part of a local church or be happy in her job or in any other environment where teamwork is necessary.

5. *Shame*: This is the emotion a person feels when he is vulnerable involuntarily, the emotion Adam and Eve felt immediately when they recognized they were naked. It is one of the core emotions that produces perfectionism and other methods employed to deny and cover up one's true state. A person who feels ashamed is inhibited in her ability to love God and to develop healthy relationships.

6. *Emotional numbness*: This state is usually a symptom of unresolved and hidden anger. The person who over anticipates being disappointed shields herself by shutting off her positive and negative emotional reactions. This affects her ability to sense God's presence, to worship Him, even to enjoy living. It renders her capable of insensitive, hurtful actions toward others, and produces a continual desire for sensational, emotional experiences. The emotionally numb person will usually gravitate toward crises or even create or escalate crises to some degree— something to stimulate her numb emotions and validate her reason for living. It is hard for crisis-oriented Christians with numb emotions to "lie down in green pastures" and chew the cud. They always have to be active.

7. *Compulsive-addictive behavior*: Many of the indulgent sins of the flesh, such as immorality, gluttony, drunkenness, and greed proceed out of addictive behavioral patterns. A Christian may have the Source of healing resident within her, but when her mind is not renewed, all efforts to resist temptations fail. She is driven repeatedly

into the addictive cycle, repeating her compulsions and feeling guilty each time. Many substance abusers substitute more acceptable addictions, such as food or work, in place of drug and alcohol addiction when they come to Christ. While they once slaved for the devil, now they slave for the Lord, driven to be active and justifying this behavior as godly.

8. *Anger*: The most often denied emotion in the Body of Christ is anger. In many circles, it is considered sinful. Gulping down this emotion in order to look more spiritual is directly responsible for emotional numbness and depression, which, next to marriage problems, are the major counseling issues dealt with in the pastor's study. Hidden anger is actually the root of bitterness talked about by the writer of Hebrews.

According to Melinda, these eight emotional issues produce the following results in the lives of Christians:

1. A distorted view of God and the inability to feel the joy of His presence.
2. The lack of joyful motivation to pray or receive comfort from prayer.
3. The inability to know and carry out the will of God for one's life.
4. The impaired ability to understand the Bible and receive comfort from its words.
5. The redefining of the first priority of the Christian life as usefulness, service, and ministry rather than worshiping and loving God.
6. The inability to make long-lasting commitments to the church, in marriage, and with friendships.[2]

Gratefully, freedom, is possible, even from the effects of our woundedness. God Himself has promised it in the words of Christ: "If you hold to my teaching, you are really my disciples. Then you will know the truth, and the truth will set you free" (John 8:31-32 NIV). The promise is emphatic. If we will believe the truth and hold to it, it will set us free from the lies of the enemy. The truth of God's love, acceptance, and approval is more powerful than the lies of rejection. Now that's news worth shouting about!

THE STRONG HELPING THE WEAK

Unfortunately, many people remain in bondage to the lies for various reasons. They need help holding on to the truth. This is why the ministry of support groups is so beneficial. For here, in a setting of love and acceptance, those who are strong in the truth help those who are weak to hold on and become strong.

Are you excited as you consider the tremendous opportunity that support group leaders have? Let the words of the Apostle Paul further encourage you:

> We who are strong ought to bear with the failings of the weak and not to please ourselves. Each of us should please his neighbor for his good, to build him up. For even Christ did not please himself but, as it is written: "The insults of those who insult you have fallen on me" (Rom. 15:1-3 NIV).

Christ's example is for us to take on those lies as our own, and strengthen one another with truth.

We have looked at the *ultimate lie* versus *the truth* as one of the key issues to understand as we seek to "know people." Women who come to your support group want to change, yet often don't realize that they are bound to lies that keep them from forgiving, healing, or changing. A privilege you have in your support group is to uncover the lies and reveal the truth that sets them free.

PEOPLE ARE THIRSTY

In the previous paragraphs we saw that people have basic needs that can be met in Christ, but because of the lies they believe, they are hindered in having these needs met. In this section we will look further into the needs of people.

Dr. Larry Crabb, founder and director of the Institute of Biblical Counseling and noted author, addresses the issue of human needs in his book *Inside Out*. He refers to the "longings" within us as that which Christ referred to when He said that He had "living water" that would satisfy and we would thirst no more. Dr. Crabb categorizes these "longings" into the following three types:

• *Crucial longings*—the basic and most profound longings of the human heart, those desires that must be met if life is to be worth living.

We were designed to live in relationship with Someone unfailingly strong and lovingly involved, who enables us to fulfill the important jobs He assigns. Nothing can satisfy our crucial longing except the kind of relationships only God offers.

• *Critical longings*—the legitimate and important desires for quality relationships that add immeasurably to the enjoyment of living.

Good marriage relationships, quality friendships, and responsive children, as well as affirming peer or job associates most often meet these longings.

• *Casual longings*—the desires for comforts, material and physical pleasures of life, non-relational needs[3]

THE SIN OF SELF-PROTECTION

As you can see, we are "thirsty" people. Our needs cry for fulfillment as clearly as a desert traveler pants for water. Too often, however, we have expectations for our needs to be met through sources that cannot meet them. When this happens, we fall into what Dr. Crabb calls the "sin of demandingness." We demand that life or God or people give us what we believe will meet our needs. When these demands are not met, we fall into the "sin of self-protection" so we won't feel the pain of life.[4]

Calling self-protection a sin sounds a bit harsh. It certainly did to a client of mine. This man was upset when another Christian working on a project with him hurt him in a way that evoked a familiar feeling—a hurt from his childhood. I recall his strong words: "Hey, when that guy walked toward my table in the cafeteria, I moved out of there right then. There was no way I was going to sit and eat my lunch next to him."

When I suggested that his avoidance was actually a sin of self-protection, he was not too pleased with me and said, "I don't see what's wrong with keeping myself from being hurt again."

Indeed, this reaction even sounds wise to us. Wouldn't God give us the wisdom to avoid being hurt again? Or would God give us openness and honesty with that person so we would be free to come into a mature, loving relationship with him? Or would God want to use that wound to draw us to Himself for further healing from our past?

Proverbs 14:12 speaks pointedly to our human inclination to avoid hurt: "There is a way which seems right to a man, but its end is the way to death." As tempting as it is to protect ourselves, we will only find healing in God's way of openness.

The issue of longings and our responses will present challenges in support groups. It is important to understand these issues in order to "know people," For further help in clarifying these concepts, I heartily recommend Dr. Crabb's book *Inside Out*.

A LOOK AT FEELINGS

Feelings are closely related to longings. Feelings are not right or wrong. They are a subconscious response to a circumstance. You may instantly feel hurt if someone doesn't speak to you. But how long you hold on to that feeling and what you think about yourself and/or him afterward is what can become a problem.

In support groups, feelings will be expressed often. In fact, many people come to groups because they need a place to express their feelings. An appropriate release of feelings is healthy. We only have to look at Scripture to see that godly men throughout the history of God's people have expressed their feelings—joy, anger, rage, grief, and passion.

In our groups we accept a person as she is and where she is with her feelings, but we want to help her see more than just what she feels in the situation. Feelings are just a corner of the picture. Feelings invite us to step back and see the whole canvas. What we are looking for is truth.

We referred above to a person not speaking to you. She may have actually been so distracted that she did not see you or she truly may have been ignoring you. If you seek the person out and she says she was distracted, then you know the truth and are free. If you seek her out and she is still cold, then you can resolve the matter and that sets you free once again.

FEELINGS ARE REAL

Feelings are real. We really feel our feelings, but we also do not want to give them authority in our lives. A person who gives authority to her feelings will have much distress and is open to deception from the enemy.

God never tells us not to feel. He created us with this marvelous ability. People who are not in touch with their feelings suffer a different kind of bondage; they are not fully alive.

You will have those in your groups who have "frozen feelings" and truly cannot express what they feel. Support groups are very helpful for them, for as they hear others express feelings, they begin to identify their own feelings, starting the process of "thawing out."

WHAT DO WE DO WITH FEELINGS?

The issue of feelings is what we do with them. In your group, allow for expression: this is *release*. Always allow time for a woman to express her feelings. After there is release of feelings, then encourage her to *receive*: to receive truth, compassion, comfort, love, acceptance, approval from the group and from the Lord. It is this process of exchange—releasing pain to receive love that makes all the difference.

In the following two chapters we will discuss the important steps related to handling feelings. In Chapter 10 we will discuss forgiveness which plays a big part in releasing feelings and in Section Four, Chapter 13 we'll look at Jesus in the Garden of Gethsemane, a perfect example of releasing and forgiving.

10

...

Control
and Choice

Many who come to support groups will be dealing with issues of *control*. As leaders you will need to understand control, know how it affects people's lives, and know how God views it.

Take Laura, for example. Married to a man whose addictive behavior continually brought chaos into their home, Laura typically assumed the codependent role, trying to make everything work. When the situation became unmanageable, she came in for counseling.

After listening carefully to this woman describe the pain she was in, I assured her things could change. "I hear where you are, Laura," I said, "and I believe I can help you. But we will begin the counseling by working toward change in you."

Her eyes opened wide, she cocked her head in disbelief, and leaned forward toward me. "Change me? But it's my husband who has the problem."

I smiled at this earnest young woman. "But we can't change him, Laura. He isn't here. We can only change you."

THE CONTROL MAZE

From then on I helped Laura see how much of her pain was self-imposed by what she, as a codependent, believed she had to do. For instance, when her husband didn't come home after work, she felt she had to stay home and wait on him, or if he were angry and depressed and wanted to hibernate in the house on a Sunday afternoon, she felt she and the children had to stay there with him. To her, this was being a family.

Laura was caught in a common maze of control. She felt controlled by her husband's problems. At the same time, she felt that everything was out of control and that she had to find a way to be in control. She had to hold everything together.

"What things would you rather do on a Sunday afternoon?" I asked her. Immediately she mentioned visiting friends or going to the park. "Is there any reason why you can't do these things?" (I did not want her to be set up to be abused.)

As if a light flicked on, she brightened at the possibility. "Well . . . no. I guess I could, couldn't I? I wouldn't be gone all day and it would be so much better than staying home when he is determined to be unhappy."

Laura began to make some different choices. Occasionally she went places or did things when her husband didn't come home or was depressed. She no longer felt controlled by his behaviors and moods. One day she exclaimed, "My life is so different now that I know I have choices!"

THE FREEDOM TO CHOOSE

Control is not an attribute of God. Certainly, God is very much in control; He is not anxious or fearful of what will happen in His world. He knows the end from the beginning and rests in the knowledge that His plan is unfolding as He has purposed. We could say that God is in control of

Himself, but not controlling of humanity. In love, He has given us the freedom to choose.

Imagine, the Creator God of the universe loved us enough to give us the freedom to exercise our own will! He created us with a soul, of which our will is part, along with our emotions and intellect. His intent was that as we joined ourselves to Him, the Holy Spirit within us would transcend our body and soul, and thus empower us to break free of the control of our sin nature and live in union with Him (See John 17:20-23).

FREE TO LOVE

Choice is expressed in two ways:

- Choice out of personal desire
- Choice in loving obedience to God's will.

In either case, the intent of choice is *love*.

God gave us the free will to choose so that we might experience the glorious liberty to give and receive love. Love that is compelled or demanded is not love for another, but love of self.

If God demanded our love, if He manipulated our love, then He would not be truly loving us, but loving Himself. God so loved us that He gave His only Son that we would not perish but have eternal life (See John 3:16.) Then He gives us the free will to receive this gift of love. "Giving freely" with opportunity to "receive freely" is the true expression of love.

THE DIFFERENCE BETWEEN NEED AND CHOICE

A few years ago, a Christian man came for a counseling appointment. When I asked what I could do for him, he said, "Just answer me one question. What is the difference between being a loving, caring Christian and a codependent?"

A most significant question! I knew it when I heard it. As we talked, the Lord gave me an answer for him and for all of us. The difference between being a loving, caring Christian and a codependent is the difference between two words: *need* and *choice*.

Need involves a subconscious motivation of fear:

- What will happen if I don't?
- What will they think if I do?
- No one else will.
- I have to.
- I'm afraid not to.

These fears stem from

- Performance orientation—I'm loved for what I do.
- A need to be needed—pseudo martyr.
- Fear of abandonment, rejection, etc.

Need is a result of being controlled either from within or from without.

Choice may carry out the same actions but without the control of fear. Choice is free to give, love, receive, or decide from the liberty of mind and heart. Choice is conscious thought.

Consider the following examples:

Your spouse says:	"I would really like a cup of coffee."
Need responds:	I should have known; why didn't I get it sooner?
or:	I can't drop what I'm doing, but he'll be angry if I don't.
Choice responds:	I'm tired and would like to just sit; but I don't mind getting his coffee.
or:	"I'm sorry, but I can't drop what I'm doing right now."
or:	"So would I. Please get me one, too."

Look at the subtle fear in what *need* thinks and the easy freedom in what *choice* thinks.

Many victims do not know they have choice. At the point of victimization, they were denied choice and thus carry this effect or the fear of it into the present situation.

WE DO NOT MAKE DECISIONS FOR OTHERS

In support groups, we do not make decisions for others. Instead, we help them explore options. By helping them see the possibilities, they are freer to make their own choice. To explore options means to look at as many possibilities as we can along with all of the resulting consequences. Then we ask the question, "Which can we best live with at the time and be pleasing to the Lord?"

For those who aren't used to making choices, the group helps by asking questions that reveal possible choices. For example:

One member of the group is struggling with her finances. We can ask her something like this: "Karen, what seems as if it would help more, keeping a monthly budget or getting another job?"

From this can come discussion of applying each of these options plus other options that will come from the group or Karen. But the ultimate choice must be Karen's, for she alone is going to live in the situation. The group encourages Karen that she is able (with the Lord) to make wise decisions. She needs to be supported in her ability to choose wisely.

THREE FATHERS' VOICES

Joshua helped the Israelites "explore their options." We read in Joshua 23 and 24 that Joshua is aware that he is about to go and be with the Lord. He summons the leaders of Israel together. He reminds them of all that the Lord has done for them, and then at the end of Chapter 24, he presents them with their choices:

Choose for yourselves this day whom you will serve, whether the gods which your fathers served that were on the other side of the River, or the gods of the Amorites, in whose land you dwell. But as for me and my house, we will serve the Lord (Jos. 24:15).

A father's voice has authority. Joshua revealed three fathers' voices:

1. The voice of our forefathers (I call this the voice or words we heard in our natural family.)
2. The voice of the god of this world
3. The voice of Father God

Our liberty to make choices will be directly related to which father's voice we are giving authority to in our life. If we are still listening to the negative voices from childhood or to the voice of the deceiver, our choices will be directed by fear and will result in some form of bondage. If we listen to the voice of Father God, our choice will be based on truth and love, giving us liberty before God.

Giving primary authority to any voice before God's is a form of idolatry. In our groups we emphasize the authority of the Word of God in all things.

11
...
The Challenge of Change

Support groups are places of change. In Section One we talked about the beauty shop concept of change that takes place within these groups. In this chapter we will look more at the actual issues surrounding change that people encounter in their lives.

The issues we'll examine are

- Victim recovery path
- Compound pain
- Parent-adult-child responses
- Grief
- Forgiveness
- Holiness

VICTIM RECOVERY PATH

Once a woman becomes aware that she has been a victim in some way, she will inevitably have a response. The direction of her response will make all the difference in her life. In support groups we want to help women on the recovery path to move in the direction of becoming rightly related to God and others. The Bible calls it "the path of righteousness."

The group leader needs to be familiar with the following diagram of this path. In this way she can direct the women to move toward the true liberty God has for them as well as warn them of the results of moving off the godly path.

Victim Recovery Path

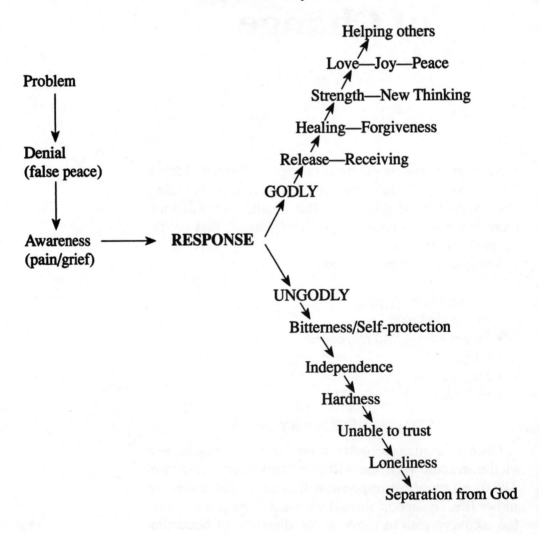

Problem

↓

Denial
(false peace)

↓

Awareness ⟶ **RESPONSE**
(pain/grief)

GODLY

Release—Receiving

Healing—Forgiveness

Strength—New Thinking

Love—Joy—Peace

Helping others

UNGODLY

Bitterness/Self-protection

Independence

Hardness

Unable to trust

Loneliness

Separation from God

It is important to note that those who desire a godly response and begin to release their feelings may sound as though they are expressing ungodly responses. Remember, all victims feel anger and injustice. The key is to not get stuck in those feelings as we saw in Chapter Nine of this section.

As the support group leader you can help by accepting the women where they are, encouraging them to receive God's grace and the support of others who understand.

Part of the very purpose of support groups is found on this recovery path, for we desire to help others move into righteous responses. The enemy wants to pull them down into what I call "being a victim of being a victim." (The downward move of the diagram reveals this trap.) When a woman takes on a victim mentality and lives as a victim, she misses out on the wonderful blessings of God's redemption and restoration.

In support groups, we work with the Holy Spirit in helping victims:

1. Let go of the past
2. Trust God
3. Move into wholeness and holiness

On the diagram, note particularly the point of response. It is here that group members will need to make a choice. As the leader, you may need to encourage them to "let go" so they can move ahead. Use this response path, then as a tool to encourage them in their choice.

THE PATTERN OF PAIN

Because support groups deal with the issues of the heart and challenge us to change, some group members may want to quit or may actually leave the group as they encounter the pain that change produces. After all, they joined the group to feel better, not to feel pain. This concept is very well explained by Dr. Chris Thurman in his book *The Lies We Believe*.

In his chapter, "The Truth About Change," Dr. Thurman reveals a pattern that breaks down into four phases. I will summarize these, using one of his examples.

Phase One   *Living in Pain*
                  My problem is that I am overweight. This has produced a level of pain that I have learned to tolerate.

Phase Two   *The Pain Worsens*
                  I decide I will lose some weight.
     1   The diet and exercise produce the added
   +2   pain of hunger and sore muscles.
  =3 Ouch!   I started with (1) form of pain, but I've added (2) more forms of pain—compound pain.
                  I want to "bail out" and go back to Phase One; I know I can tolerate that pain.

Phase Three   *From Pain to Pleasure*
                  I see some results of my dieting and exercise.
                  I still have to work hard, though, and am tempted to go back.
                  But I feel some hope and encouragement.

Phase Four   *The Plateau*
                  I've reached my goal and feel great. I still have some pain, though, the pain of maintaining my goal.

Compound pain occurs in phase two, and you can easily recognize the pattern of defeat that occurs with this added pain. Dr. Thurman says, "Phase two is so difficult that we all need tremendous support and encouragement to get through it."[1] This is exactly why many people join support groups. Weight Watchers and AA are two prominent examples of how this works.

TIME FOR ENCOURAGEMENT

Many people are still surprised by the degrees of pain they will encounter with change and some may actually "bail out." If you notice that group members have been absent, reaching out to them and asking about the pain may be the support they need. Sometimes they don't leave the group, but they begin to criticize the group or the leader. It is their way of saying, "Being here hurts." They are resisting their own change by thinking that if the group or leader would change then they would feel better.

Explaining the concept of compound pain can help the group persevere. It also helps to encourage them with the truth: that the pain lessens and actually becomes a positive force as eternal change begins to take place. We might say that it is a bit like coaching a mother through labor and delivery. We stand by eagerly and say: "You can do it." "Not much longer." "It'll be worth it!"

If someone does drop out of the group because of the pain, you have not failed. The pain is real. At another time she may be more able to endure it.

DEDICATED TO THE TRUTH

Dr. Thurman concludes by saying, "The answer to whether or not you stay in phase four will be tied to whether or not you stay dedicated to the truth."[2] For some who want to quit, this may be an issue.

Often people hold a variety of beliefs about the process: God shouldn't make it hard; it isn't fair if it hurts; if they just have enough faith it will change; that it's God's responsibility to change them and therefore they have no responsibility in the process.

One of my clients was in great denial and when I confronted him about the need to do something differently, he continually said, "Oh, I know. I've been praying for God to help me with that." This is avoidance behavior.

He avoided being responsible for change by making God responsible to help him. The truth is that through the Holy Spirit we are already empowered to live for Christ. There is nothing more the Lord must do. It is now our turn. Perhaps you can relate it to driving a car. God has provided the engine and the gasoline, but we must put the key in the ignition and step on the gas.

As Dr. Thurman says, we must be dedicated to the truth of God's enabling power and the truth that His plan of change is good. (See Jeremiah 29:11 and Philippians 4:13.)

PARENT-ADULT-CHILD

Another common "people issue" that occurs in relationships and may occur among members of your group is the role interaction of parent-adult-child or P-A-C. Within each of us we have all three.

We all have parents who gave us the do's and don'ts as we grew up. We retain those parental injunctions. Some of us retain more of this parental nature than others. If we become parents ourselves we will repeat these messages and attitudes.

THE PARENTAL ROLE

"Parenting" is appropriate and beneficial between a parent and a child. But problems arise when adults retain too much of the parental attitude and parent other adults.

Parental messages are familiar to all of us:

You *need* to . . .
Why *haven't* you . . . ?
You *should.*
You *shouldn't.*
Don't you think you *ought to?*
You *must.*

The italicized words are common "parental words." Listen to yourself. You'll be amazed at how often you will give these parental messages to those around you. In fact, marriages are often affected by one of the partners being too parental with the other.

As support group leaders we are careful not to use "parental words" and we want to caution the group not to use these with one another.

It is essential that you do not assume a parental attitude as a group leader. You are not there to "shape them up."

As the leader, you are to relate adult to adult. When this does not occur, the group will fail; those who don't want to be parented will leave, and you will be left with dependent people who will burn you out as you try to "take care" of so many at once.

THE CHILD ROLE

The opposite of being the parent, of course, is to be the child. Some people want to be "parented"; they are passive and dependent on others caring for them. Others will become the argumentative "child" if someone else is too parental and enter into blame-shifting to avoid adult responsibility. This happens often in alcoholic homes when the wife tries to get the husband to change. She plays the mother role and he the rebellious teenager.

THE ADULT ROLE

In support groups we encourage all members to be responsible for themselves, and we support them in making their own decisions and accepting the consequences. This is the adult role.

The "adult" is the one who hears the parental messages and feels the child within but makes the appropriate choices. Our adult is responsible to filter the messages from the P-A-C within and the P-A-C messages from others and make the appropriate choice. By this I mean that it may be just fine to listen to the child within and play rather than work at times or it may be important to finish your work before you play. The "adult," through maturity, can discern a bigger picture and choose.

Because of being in strong parenting relationships, some in your group may not have developed their "adult" within. Support group will be challenging for them in this area. Those who are strongly parental will be challenged to let others choose and even challenged to play more themselves. Those who have a strong "child" will learn to live less from their feelings and to take responsibility.

AN EXAMPLE OF FREEDOM

I have a friend who does not play easily and the "little girl" in me used to drive her crazy. She kept wanting me to "behave." I learned from her to be a bit more appropriate, but mostly she was challenged by me to have more fun. Her "parent" and my "child" were once a problem for each other, but now we are both freer as adults because we let the Lord use our understanding of P-A-C to help us both grow. Hopefully, this will take place in your groups.

THE ISSUE OF GRIEF

People in our culture generally have very little understanding or compassion for the grieving process. Not so Jesus. The prophet Isaiah speaking prophetically described Him as the Messiah-to-come, "despised and rejected by men, a Man of sorrows and acquainted with grief" (Isa. 53:3). In Jesus' time, grief was acknowledged as a necessary process of life, and room was given for it to be expressed. In our time and culture, there is little tolerance given for grieving, thus we often don't recognize when we are grieving or why we are grieving.

Let me offer a definition of grief:

Grief is simply defined as sorrow.
Grief is felt when any form of change takes place.

Even when change is positive, such as moving to a new home or going to college or getting married, sorrow may be felt, for we must leave one part of our life to have the other.

Take the example of one of my clients: She couldn't understand why she was depressed. After all, her dream had finally come through: she and her husband had sold their home and moved into a new retirement home. This was what they'd planned for a long time. "Why I am so upset?" she asked me. "All of this should make me happy!"

"You are feeling the goodbyes." I told her. As we talked, she began to let herself feel some of the grief over all those accumulated experiences and memories in her old home.

"I do so miss going into my daughter's old bedroom. She'll never be a little girl in our new house. I like my kitchen, but I keep reaching for the old cabinets." She was feeling the grief of change, the letting go of the old in order to have the new.

We tend to think of grief in terms of death and change indeed involves death: the death of what was, and the death of what could have been.

GRIEF IS A PROCESS

Experts on grief mostly agree that it is a process that involves stages. There are variations on these stages, but we will look at the most commonly acknowledged study on death and dying done by Elizabeth Kubler-Ross. She presents these stages:

1. Denial
2. Anger
3. Bargaining
4. Depression
5. Acceptance[3]

Now, for a closer look at each stage.

Denial   — Does not acknowledge what has hap-
             pened or is happening. I'm fine. I'm not
             upset.
Anger   — Feels the pain and wants to hurt back.
             How could God let this happen?
             It's not fair.
             This shouldn't have happened.
Bargaining — Attempts or wishes they could change
             the truth.
             If only . . .
             Maybe if I . . .
             God, I promise . . .
Depression — Feels hopeless and overwhelmed.
             Nothing will ever be the same.
             I don't know if I can go on.
             Life is too hard.
Acceptance — With sadness, lets go.
             Acknowledges what they cannot change.
             Accepts the pain of loss.

These stages of grief are necessary. God doesn't require us to take the full impact of loss all at once, but through grace gives us this process so the pain comes in manageable doses.

I like Dr. Timothy Foster's comments on grief. He says, "Maybe you don't believe in magic words, but in the process of handling grief, there is one word with almost magical properties, the word *goodbye*. Goodbye is the period at the end of the earthly relationship with a person."[4] This can also be said of the end of anything—a marriage, a job, a living situation. There needs to be a closure of some kind. I agree with Dr. Foster that *goodbye* works very well.

SAYING GOODBYE

Grief is the process of saying goodbye. When that word is deliberately and audibly used, it truly brings release. I have often had clients write letters saying goodbye to people who had not been in their lives for a long time. Or they go to the Lord in prayer to say goodbye to things that must be forsaken.

I had the Lord personally minister this to me several years ago. I had been emotionally dependent in a relationship, and when that person moved out of my life, I thought I would die from the grief. One day as I was sobbing out my loss, I cried to the Lord, "When will I ever quit crying?" He lovingly answered, "Crying is letting go." From that moment on whenever I wept I would say, "I let go! I let go! I let go!" and simultaneously the grief began to subside. The Lord taught me to say, *Goodbye*.

GIVING COMFORT IN GRIEF

Dr. Foster also says, "People who are hurting need your caring and support, not your sermons, lectures, or condemnations."[5] This was the Lord's way with me. The emotional dependency I was in was idolatry, but when I wept, He did not condemn me for my sin; He showed me how to say goodbye. He showed me how to work with the grief process and be free to go on with His wonderful plan for my life.

As support group leaders we want to follow our Lord's example and comfort those who grieve, gently showing them how to say goodbye.

12

. . .

The Reality
of Change

One of the greatest satisfactions a support group leader can have is to observe growth and change in those coming to the group. You'll know it when you see it: women who once came to the group feeling defeated and discouraged are now able to look one another in the eye; they feel acceptable, loved, and at peace. God's truth has conquered Satan's lies and they are "living proof" that the life of Christ is now finding fuller expression within them.

Part of that expression will most likely be found in *forgiveness* and *holiness*, two significant aspects of change. Let's look first at forgiveness.

THE CHALLENGE TO FORGIVE

When we look at the biblical examples, we can hardly believe we could ever forgive in like manner. There was Stephen, a man like us, who in the face of being stoned to death, cries out, "Lord, do not charge them with this sin" (Acts 7:60). Such love seems incredible.

And of course there was Jesus. In excruciating pain, with death descending, He cried out to God: "Father, forgive them, for they do not know what they do" (Luke 23:34). How could anyone forgive like this?

Christ in us is able!

LOOKING AT UNFORGIVENESS

Because many who are in support groups have been hurt, used, abused, abandoned, or deceived by some significant person or persons, forgiveness will definitely arise as an issue in your group. For most people, forgiveness is something they know they must grant, but they stumble over actually granting it, or even knowing how.

Forgiveness can also be delayed because of misconceptions about what is actually involved. I believe the following explanations of unforgiveness and forgiveness will be helpful.

Unforgiveness is a choice we make when

- It is an attempt to control—to have my own way.
- It refuses to accept what has happened, release it to God, and believe in His goodness.
- It is my attempt to be God. All my "shoulds" rule my heart:

    They shouldn't have said. . . .
    She shouldn't have done . . . .
    It shouldn't have happened. . . .
    They should pay. . . .

- It holds me captive to what has happened in the past while others live in the joy of the present.
- It binds my wounds to me when God would heal.
- It is really my anger at God that He allowed me to be hurt, used, rejected. I'm stamping my foot at Him and saying, "How could you let this happen to me?"
- It believes in punishment, that if I forgive then no one will be punished.

- It believes that forgiving is saying that what was done was all right.

Unforgiving people feel justified because

- They have *really* been hurt.
- They believe that the other person deserves to be punished for what they have done and they can't forgive until this happens.

To help a person in your group with unforgiveness, you can ask questions about what it is costing them emotionally, mentally, physically, and spiritually. Many who hold unforgiveness have admitted to a vast array of physical symptoms of stress: headaches, arthritis, ulcers, high blood pressure, insomnia, irritable bowels, and fatigue.

Their emotional symptoms of anxiety include: depression, mental symptoms of lack of concentration, compulsive behaviors, and memory loss.

Their spiritual symptoms include: lack of joy, diminished interest in prayer, Bible study, and fellowship, a sense that God is far off.

Unforgiveness exacts a high price!

LOOKING AT FORGIVENESS

A friend told me about a life-changing event that took place at a support group meeting during a discussion on forgiveness. She had just finished sharing her frustration at feeling "stuck" in unforgiveness toward her mother-in-law. The whole process somehow just didn't work for her.

Wisely, patiently, the leader drew her out, finally posing a pointed question: "Have you thought about just making a choice to forgive?" That's where we begin with forgiveness—making a choice.

Forgiveness is a choice we make when

- We love God more than ourselves.
- We desire to be righteous in the sight of God rather than "right" in the eyes of man.
- We believe in God's love.
- We desire to love as Christ loved us.

Forgiveness is

- A decision of the heart.
- The heart's desire to love God and others no matter what.
- Embracing the life of the cross.
- Losing your life that you might find your life.
- The only way we are ever totally free.

Forgiveness lets God be God and trusts in His divine justice, mercy, and goodness. It is not something we understand logically.

FORGIVENESS IS A PROCESS

The process of forgiving involves making a choice to let go, to remove the offending person from our judgment, and to release him from any responsibility, trusting God to be the justifier.

But what do we do with our feelings when they don't line up to our choice? The answer is, we STAND strong in our choice to forgive. We are not tossed to and fro by our feelings. Feelings will eventually come into submission to our will. And while we're waiting, we can choose to "bless our enemies" (See Romans 12:17-21). We can't deny that God's clear call to forgive insists on a changed heart toward the one who has hurt us.

As women in support groups share and take responsibility for their feelings and behavior, they inevitably bump up against the biblical boundaries. It is sinners who need forgiveness, and the more we honestly see ourselves as sinners saved by grace, the easier it truly is to forgive others.

Jesus Himself strongly challenged us on the issue of forgiveness. "For if you forgive men when they sin against you, your heavenly Father will also forgive you. But if you do not forgive men their sins, your Father will not forgive your sins" (Matt. 6:14). To have eternal life, it is necessary to be forgiven; to be forgiven, it is necessary to forgive.

Peace with God is found as we are at peace with man. The unforgiving person has no peace with God.

FORGIVENESS IS OUR GREATEST WEAPON

A special friend who has endured much rejection and pain in her marriage said that she has learned from God that forgiveness is our greatest weapon. With it, we bind the work of the enemy and we loose ourself and the other person for God to work by His grace in us. Knowing that forgiveness defeats the enemy is strong motivation. It helps us release our anger in a righteous direction.

Forgiveness, she discovered, began with a willingness to forgive. If we don't feel willing, then we can tell the Lord we are willing to be made willing. God will meet us where we are. This can be useful in leading support groups to help those who struggle with unforgiveness to move into willingness.

It will be important to encourage group members that we grow in our ability to forgive. As we mature we forgive at different levels. At the point of willingness, we may forgive on a very basic level, but as we grow in Christ we will forgive that same person on deeper and deeper levels. Forgiveness is not a one time prayer, but more often, a progressive expression of grace.

When unforgiveness is expressed in our support groups, we are to lovingly confront it with Christ's words from Matthew 6:14-15 and encourage the women to begin praying at their point of willingness.

THE CALL TO HOLINESS

For Christians, the ultimate goal of change is holiness,

that we might be like Jesus. That we might be holy as He is holy. Listen to this same emphasis from Scripture:

Make every effort to live in peace with all men and to be holy; without holiness no one will see the Lord (Heb. 12:14 NIV).

And:

But just as he who called you is holy, so be holy in all you do; for it is written: "Be holy, because I am holy" (1 Pet. 1:15-16 NIV).

All change in our lives should be pointed toward the goal of being holy as Jesus is holy. Most of us feel like Paul, that we haven't arrived. But like Paul, we must be pressing on toward the prize (Phil. 3:12-14). Often people who are in the process of change lose sight of the purpose. Some get so involved in the process that the process becomes the goal. As support group leaders we need to gently and consistently remind the group that the purpose of change is holiness; we are being transformed into the likeness of Christ.

WHOLENESS/HOLINESS

We are not changing so we will have a better life, be happier, be whole, or be free. These are all side benefits to the true goal of change. We seek to change so that we may be holy. "For he chose us in him before the creation of the world to be holy and blameless in his sight." (Eph. 1:4 NIV).

Wholeness is a term used by much of the world today with various connotations. A desire for wholeness is not sinful. In fact, throughout the Gospels in the King James Version of Scripture, when Jesus heals, the term, *made whole* is used. The key is that we do not seek wholeness in some worldly sense, but we seek holiness. Wholeness in itself is self-satisfying; holiness is God-satisfying. Wholeness will be found in holiness.

Holiness becomes the plumb line by which we as support group leaders assess the results of change in our groups. By this I mean that we encourage the group members to move through change and make decisions based upon that which pleases God rather than pleasing self or others. We are not looking for outward expressions of holiness, but for the devoted heart.

Because holiness is a desire of the heart, it cannot be taught or produced. But holiness can be seen and this seeing can ignite desire. Seek as a leader to let the passion for holiness in your own life be that spark that becomes a guiding light for the group.

A FINAL WORD ON CHANGE

Change, whether it be in worldly circumstances or within our own hearts, has been ordained by God to bring forth His plan of redemption. First we see it within each of us, then upon the earth, then throughout all creation. Thus, whatever effects come with change, we can say, "And we know that all things work together for good to those who love God, to those who are the called according to His purpose" (Rom. 8:28).

With all the uncertainty change produces, we are made secure by the truth that, " 'Though the mountains be shaken and the hills be removed, yet my unfailing love for you will not be shaken nor my covenant of peace be removed' says the Lord who has compassion on you" (Isa. 54:10). Hallelujah, the Lord changes not!

You have now completed the reading in Section Three. Please turn to the worksheets for this section on page 212, and reproduce a copy. Then fill in your answers on the copy. If you are applying to become an Aglow support group leader, mail your completed sheets to Jennie Newbrough at the address on page 202. Be sure to include a stamped, self-addressed, business size (#10) envelope to facilitate their return. If you are reading for your own edification, you also may want to reproduce the worksheets, fill them in, and keep them as part of your self-study.

Section IV

Know Support Groups

THE PRIVILEGE   of this section is to see the distinctive characteristics of support groups.

THE CHALLENGE   of this section is to grasp hold of these dynamics personally.

13

...

The Anatomy of a Support Group

They are everywhere—hurting, wounded people. People desperately looking for freedom from the effects of their own sins or the sins committed against them. Many of them know that God offers more than they are experiencing, but they don't know how to find it.

In Chapter One of this book we looked in on some women who found a "safe place" to expose their wounds. They were gathered in Karen's family room on a Monday night, supporting one another and allowing God's love and truth to be applied as a salve for their healing.

There in that confidential, safe place, the women talked about walls they'd built to protect themselves from further hurt and pain. They shared their feelings truthfully and then, by evening's end, made choices to receive Christ's truth to counter their wrong beliefs. We saw support group ministry in action.

In this three-chapter section, we'll be taking a closer look at support groups. We want to understand fully how these groups work. In this first chapter, we'll observe how support groups function as safe places, the different concepts of what they are, and the leadership styles that facilitate them.

JESUS HAD A SAFE PLACE

One day a thought from the Lord captured my attention: *A great deal of the American church would have denied me Gethsemane.*

What was Gethsemane? We know it was a public garden east of Jerusalem, near the Mount of Olives, the place where Jesus went before He was arrested and taken away by the Roman soldiers. But it was much more.

This was the place Jesus needed so he could feel His pain. Here He could say, "Father, I am afraid. Father; if it is possible, don't make me go through this! Father, hear me!" He needed a place to release His emotions and fears, to empty Himself of feelings in order to receive the grace of His Father. Christ needed Gethsemane, and God provided.

As I meditated on Gethsemane, I recalled Jesus' deep heart-wrenching cry, "My soul is overwhelmed with sorrow to the point of death" (Matt. 26:38). His intense agony caused him to sweat drops of blood. And what did His Father do? He listened and comforted His Son; He let Him release the agony of His soul. He sent an angel to comfort Him.

I realized that the Father responded differently to His Son's anguish, than the Church often responds to the anguish of our souls. The Father did not say: "What kind of example are you being for the disciples? Where is your faith? I thought I could trust you to be strong. You're being controlled by your emotions. Get hold of yourself."

No. God didn't tell Jesus to have more faith, pray more, or stand on the Word. He listened and comforted and let His Son release His soul's agony. Then, in the releasing, came the strength to choose obedience.

THE NEED FOR SUPPORT

Jesus did not want to be alone in Gethsemane. More than once He pleaded with His disciples to pray and be His support. If our Lord, who was filled with the Holy Spirit, needed a "safe place" and support how much more we who are yet being filled need a Gethsemane place and support.

Far too often hurting people have nowhere to go with their emotions. No one offers a place to release what hurts—to talk out their emotions—to express their fears. Consequently, many times hurting people simply don't work through their pain to receive God's healing grace.

Here is where support group ministry comes in. Drawing the parallel of Jesus in Gethsemane, we can say that these groups are gardens for the soul, and the comforting "angels" sent by God are those of us who give support.

DIFFERENT CONCEPTS OF SUPPORT GROUPS

There are many types of support groups functioning in very different ways and offering various kinds of support. None is right or wrong, better or worse. Support groups function with different formats in order to achieve specific goals. The goal of the group will be a determining factor in choosing the type of group.

We want to distinguish Aglow's concept of support groups from other group concepts. Many people confuse Bible studies or share groups with support groups. Bible studies are focused on learning the Word of God; share groups are focused on individuals sharing whatever happens to be on their minds at the time; support groups are focused on the felt needs of members who are dealing with the same specific life issue.

In *Rapha's Handbook for Group Leaders* four types of groups are explored according to purpose:

- *Task groups* exist to complete a project, plan a retreat, or organize fund raising.

- *Teaching groups* exist to impart knowledge, give instructions, classes, seminars, Bible studies
- *Growth groups* exist to encourage and challenge to grow, discipleship
- *Support groups* exist to give strength and care, healing, recovery[1]

DEFINING AGLOW SUPPORT GROUPS

Aglow support groups are a blend of these different kinds. Our focus is on growth with support, and there is some biblical teaching involved. The following statements from the *Aglow Leader's Digest* define support groups.

Support groups are

- Compassionate, non-threatening, confidential places where people can be open about their struggles and receive caring and support in a biblically-based, Christ-centered atmosphere.
- An accepting place where people are listened to and loved right where they are.
- A place where love and truth are shared and the Holy Spirit is present to bring God's healing.
- A place where people learn to take responsibility for making Christ-like choice in their own lives.

Support groups are not

- Counseling groups
- Places to "fix" or change someone
- Bible studies or prayer groups, although scripture and prayer are used
- Places where people concentrate on themselves and "stay there." Instead, they provide opportunity to grow in self-responsibility and wholeness in Christ.[2]

RESPONSIBLE CAUTIONS

Having traveled as Aglow's U.S. support group resource person for three years, I have talked with many people, both Christians and non-Christians, about support groups and am very aware of the differing concepts about them.

Some associate support groups with "encounter groups" that were popular in secular circles in the '60s and '70s or other types of professional therapy groups. Some fear that Christianity is being deceived by New Age thinking and the popular self-help and Twelve Step group concepts of today.

I listen well to these comments, for I believe caution is a responsible reaction. After all, Scripture tells us to test every spirit and to be aware because if possible Satan will deceive even the very elect.

AGLOW'S PERSPECTIVE

Aglow believes that support groups provide one way for the Body of Christ to fulfill its call to build itself up in love into all things in Christ Jesus (Eph.4:12-13). We all know someone (perhaps even ourself) who has had an issue that continually affects her life, one she has had prayer for many times, but it is still there. Support group is that safe place to work through the emotions and fears surrounding this life issue, to receive healing and be strengthened, and to get to the root and fully focus on overcoming it.

OTHER FORMATS

A few years ago, Dr. David (Paul) Youngi Cho from Seoul, Korea, impacted the Church with the concept of home cell groups. Tremendous growth has taken place in his church as well as other churches world-wide who have adapted a version of home groups.

Aglow's concept of support groups is not an adaptation of home groups. Our support groups deal with specific life issues—heart issues. But our groups do result in the same growth and Christian discipleship that is experienced in home groups.

The success of home groups reveals that people want places to grow and change. Not everyone has a church offering this opportunity. Aglow, however, is available to believers and non-believers, regardless of church affiliation. At the same time, Aglow works in one accord with the local Body of Christ to provide for the needs of its people.

MAINTAINING THE AGLOW FORMAT

It is important that we thoroughly define our concept of support groups for Aglow so that we can maintain continuity and accountability in the ministry. As we mentioned earlier in the book, for those who desire to lead Aglow support groups this will mean that you must be willing to lay aside the format and ways you may have learned or experienced in other groups. We recognize that they worked well for you and we do not discredit them, but the Aglow format may differ in some ways.

Alcoholics Anonymous and other help groups have formats which are fine for them but may differ somewhat from what we advocate. We are not in competition with these groups but seek to fill the place God has called Aglow to in this area of ministry.

Aglow is unique in its outreach and ministry, and our support groups must correlate with this overall ministry. When leading an Aglow support group, we require that you adopt the Aglow format.

OTHER AREAS FOR SUPPORT

Support can take place in many groups that are not actually support groups. Many Aglow boards, local and area, offer support to the officers. Many people have small prayer groups or Bible studies that offer an atmosphere where there is open sharing and support. These are all good, but they are not what we are defining as support groups.

Outreach groups, though supportive by nature, are not

support groups. The Aglow ministry encourages outreach into the community of various kinds; clothes closets, fellowship in housing developments, prison ministry, etc. These groups offer support to struggling people, but they do not offer the kind of support we refer to in support groups.

LEADERSHIP STYLE: MODERATOR OR FACILITATOR?

Leadership style is a factor that is a great determiner of support group concepts. Two styles most frequently used are *moderating* and *facilitating*.

The moderator: When a leader is functioning as a moderator, she functions according to the dictionary definition of *moderate*, which is "observing, restrained, not extreme in opinion, implied absence or avoidance of excess." All this means is that she offers little guidance or input; basically she just oversees the meeting. With the moderating style there is no confrontation; members take turns sharing their thoughts with little interaction between the group members and from the leader. This moderating style allows the freedom to express what you want in an accepting environment.

The facilitator: The facilitating style of leadership is much more interactive. From *Theory and Practice of Group Counseling* by Gerald Corey, we get our definition of facilitating:

Facilitating is aimed at enhancing the group experience and enabling the members to reach their goals. Facilitation skills involve opening up clean and direct communication among the participants and helping them assume increasing responsibility for the direction of the group.

Gerald Corey gives specific ways group leaders facilitate. These are listed below:

- Focusing on resistance within the group and helping members realize when they are holding back and why
- Encouraging members to openly express their feelings and expectations

- Teaching members to focus on themselves and their feelings
- Actively working to create a climate of safety that will encourage members to take risks
- Providing support for members as they try new behaviors
- Fostering a member-to-member, rather than member-to-leader interaction style
- Encouraging open expression of conflict
- Assisting members in overcoming barriers to direct communication
- Helping members integrate what they are learning in the group and finding ways to apply it to their everyday lives
- Helping members achieve closure by taking care of any unfinished business in the group[3]

AGLOW'S LEADERSHIP STYLE

Facilitating is the leadership style to be used for Aglow support groups. This style works with our goals for growth and support and with the materials used in our groups. Facilitating does require more from the leader, and that is why we have this training material.

A young woman I know had overcome her painful childhood. As part of her new freedom to play, she had actually chosen to parasail while she and her husband were on an anniversary trip to the Bahamas. When she returned, she was scheduled to begin leading an Aglow support group. Showing me her parasailing photos, she exclaimed: "You know, leading the support group is more frightening than parasailing!" You may identify with her as you look at the above facilitating responsibilities.

FACILITATING IS WORK

Facilitating is indeed a challenging responsibility. In fact, it is work. Yet it is very gratifying. The group leader is "fully present" at all times, listening, observing, involving others, questioning, guiding, encouraging, comforting, praying, caring. This is why I say that you must WORK, not just read Sections Four and Five of this training guide.

Just to read the material will not make it part of you. You will become a successful group facilitator as you work the concepts. Practice with friends, pray for God's enabling in these areas, concentrate on learning these skills that may be new for you. It is a bit like applying for a new job and receiving job training for the specific work you were hired to do. Because facilitating a support group is different from other forms of ministry, you will acquire new job skills. These skills will be examined in full in Section Five.

SUMMARY OF AGLOW'S SUPPORT GROUP CONCEPT

In review, let's summarize Aglow's concept of what our support groups offer:

1. Opportunity—for women to share openly and honestly their struggles and pain over a specific issue in a non-judgmental, Christ-centered framework.

2. Safe Place—for women to gain perspective on mutual problems and begin taking responsibility for themselves.

3. Atmosphere—that is compassionate, confidential, understanding, and committed to challenging participants from a biblical perspective.

Our **goal** of growth and support is *discipleship*.
Our **style** of leadership is *facilitating*.
Our **purpose** is to *support* one another to live according to the Lord and His righteousness.

14
...
Group Guidelines

Have you ever watched a curious child taking something apart? Maybe it's a little appliance or a complicated toy— something with nuts, bolts, and wheels that spin. Then, surprise! Mom appears on the scene and the child, surrounded by dozens of screws and strange metal pieces, looks up and says innocently, "I just want to see how it works."

That's what we want to find out about support groups. What are the "nuts and bolts" that keep these groups running?

How do they function and what are their distinctive dynamics? We're going to take an inside look.

GROUP SIZE

Support group size is very important. I recommend between three and twelve women. This allows time for all to share and for intimacy and trust to grow. If more than twelve come, you will have some choices to make. The following are options:

1. Split the group when it is interaction time. This requires at least one additional leader.

2. Form two separate groups, with an additional leader.

3. Have some wait for another group to start up.

MEETING FREQUENCY AND LENGTH

Support group purpose is best achieved when the group meets consistently: weekly or bi-monthly.

An hour and a half is the appropriate length of time for a support group. The following reasons help clarify this guideline:

- Leaders cannot be "fully present" for much longer.
- Members will be encouraged to attend regularly if time is consistent.
- Probing into sensitive areas for too long can become uncomfortable.
- Discipline is important to the group.
- This schedule keeps the format flowing.

OPEN/CLOSED GROUP TYPES

Support groups can be open or closed. An open group means that new people can join the group at any time. A closed group means that after the first two or three meetings, no new person may join the group. Whether a group is open or closed can be determined by the leader and/or group. Note the advantages and disadvantages of each:

Open
Can be disruptive
Can inhibit trust factor
Can stimulate and encourage
Some adjustment of material use required
Not appropriate for sensitive subject areas i.e. sexual abuse
Some leaders may be uncomfortable with this.

Closed
Promotes trust and openness

Facilitates moving toward goal
Can prevent people who truly need this kind of group from joining and receiving help

APPROPRIATE MEETING PLACES

Because support groups are safe places, the meeting place needs to be carefully chosen. Note the following:

- A small, private, comfortable room where seating can be arranged is ideal.
- Seating in a circle or semi-circle is necessary. Seating should be as comfortable as possible.
- Very public places—hotels, open community rooms— are not acceptable.
- Private homes may be acceptable if there are no interruptions from family or phone calls. If family members' presence threatens confidentiality, this is not an appropriate safe place.
- Often churches have classrooms or meeting rooms that work well.
- Room must be available on a consistent basis.

TOPICS

There are several ways to determine what the group's topic should be. Consider the following:

1. Obvious needs as seen in people's lives
2. Praying for God-known needs to form a group around
3. Researching to determine a "needs analysis" of community
4. Is a skilled leader available for specific issue?

HOW TO LET OTHERS KNOW ABOUT A NEW GROUP FORMING

Often leaders or sponsoring groups are unsure how to let people know about their group. Consider the following:

1. Announce at fellowship meetings. Perhaps have a group leader talk.
2. Use all free public advertising available—newspaper, TV, radio, bookstores.
3. Contact pastors, other Christian leaders. Christian and secular counselors are often looking for credible groups to which they can refer clients.
4. Word-of-mouth is the most effective advertising.
5. Remember that your group will be limited in size so you may want to have a contact phone number in your advertising.
6. Date, time, location, and topic are to be clearly presented in all advertising.

WHO SHOULD BE IN A GROUP?

A friend with a master's degree in counseling told me that she didn't know anyone who would not benefit from a support group. I agree. However, people need to be encouraged to honor their individual needs. Not every group or every time is right for everyone! Note the following as to who should and who should not be in a group.

Who would benefit from a group:

- Those dealing with the same heart issue
- Those desiring godly change in their lives
- Those emotionally and mentally able to become responsible for self

Who would not benefit from a group:

- Those who do not have the "heart issue" in their personal life (no curious observers allowed)
- Those who mentally or emotionally are unable to become responsible for themselves
- Those who are resistant or disruptive to the group process
- Those receiving counseling or therapy whose counselor

feels they are not ready for group work; counseling and the group sessions should complement one another.

WHEN TO SUGGEST REFERRALS

Any support group, whether it's an Aglow or other Christ-centered group, is not designed to "cure" everyone. Our groups are not designed to handle people with severe situations and/or mental and emotional conditions. Accept this and relax in your limitations.

However, you may wish to refer these people to other avenues of help. Remember that we do not exist to "fix" others. We are not counselors.

The group leader should compile a list of credible resource people: counselors, pastors, recovery centers, etc., that can be given to those in the group when needed.

Here are some behaviors that indicate a need for referral. The key issue with these is that the behaviors are extreme and persistent.

- Extreme anger, hostility, rage
- Suicidal comments of any kind
- Expressions of despair, hopelessness, depression that are on-going
- Aggressive, domineering, controlling manner that persists
- Extreme weight loss or gain or on-going comments about eating habits
- Inability to concentrate, mentally distracted
- Comments that reveal abusive treatment of others

Referral means that the person would benefit from professional help. Suggesting referral does not always mean that the person cannot remain in the group. This depends on how disruptive her behavior is for others.

If you must suggest referral, do it gently and privately. Some people will be relieved to be offered help; others may become defensive and feel rejected. If their response is negative, affirm that you are just making a suggestion and ask that they think about it and take it to prayer. Lovingly check back and follow up with them.

If they refuse to seek help and their behavior hinders the group, you may need to release them from the group. You cannot allow one person's problem to control the group.

USING CO-LEADERS

Having two leaders for a group is ideal. One could be considered the *active leader*, taking the primary leadership, and the other the *support leader*, the one assisting. If both are experienced, then they may choose to take turns from week to week. If the support leader is just learning, she will want to maintain that role and assist the active leader. Having two leaders has many advantages:

The leaders work together with the group and the active leader benefits by having someone to assess the group dynamics and her leadership skills. The co-leader is there to support the active leader while the active leader has the responsibility for all information given and for the flow of the group, unless she delegates.

All support group leaders are servant leaders, modeling right relationships. The co-leader is never to compete with the active leader. Any difference of opinion or disagreement should be handled privately or with other Aglow leaders outside of group time.

The group does not exist for the leadership. If the leaders cannot resolve their problem, then the co-leader should leave the group. It could be she would work well with another active leader or opt to serve at another time.

SUPPORT GROUP MATERIAL

Aglow support groups use materials that address the heart issue the group is dealing with. We recommend these materials:

• Aglow *Heart Issues* books—These books on a variety of topics have been written specifically to be used in support groups. The format is designed to help group members identify their issue, and challenge them to grow, and also to assist the group leader in imparting information and asking the appropriate questions.

• Other approved materials—There are many excellent books on topics important to support groups. We ask that Aglow leaders contact the U.S. fellowships department for approval of non-Aglow materials. Note: Leaders need to be aware that much secular material, though good in information, is humanistic in application.

Materials may be used in a variety of ways:

1. Ideally, every group member has a book and uses it to prepare for each group session.
2. If group members do not or cannot buy the books then the leader must impart the information by summarizing or highlighting and give verbal homework assignments.
3. The group can also cover the material or parts of it together in the group.
4. The material offers an outline for the group that can be adapted to the needs of the group.
5. The material is only a springboard to group discussion, and teaching it or reviewing it should not dominate the group time.

A current list of Aglow *Heart Issues* support group books is given at the end of this book.

THE OFFERING

Aglow support group sessions provide a welcome opportunity to give to the Lord and His ministries. Occasionally, a basket may be passed or placed in a set location. Any offerings are to be given to your local Aglow treasurer.

PERSONAL MINISTRY

An interesting dynamic occurs in support groups when people express hurt or emotion. The Body of Christ is accustomed to immediately praying for the person, but in the group we let them feel their pain and save needed ministry until the close of group time. Group leaders and members with strong mercy motives find this difficult to adjust to.

When someone is expressing feelings, reach out a hand for comfort or say that you know they are hurting, but don't short-circuit what the Lord is doing by inserting ministry just then. Offer to pray with them at the close of the meeting.

Holding ministry until the end of the meeting has two purposes:

1. It allows the woman to work through her pain and to let the process work in her. Often she may not need prayer because the release and what was brought forth in group was what she actually needed.

2. It disciplines the group to honor the group format and allows those who must leave on time to do so without feeling they have missed group time.

SUPPORT GROUP GUIDELINES

It is important that all group members know the "ground rules" for support group. We have seen that support groups are different from other groups and from one another, so it is vital for group member to have guidelines to follow. These should be read or reviewed at *every* group session. You may want to have a member read them at the opening of each session.

These guidelines are in the back of every Aglow *Heart Issues* book. If you are using non-Aglow material or if everyone does not have a book, simply make copies for the group of the Aglow guidelines below. (You will also find some of these guidelines in the *Leader's Digest*).

BASIC SUPPORT GROUP GUIDELINES

1. You have come to give and receive support. No "fixing." We are to listen, support, and be supported by one another, not give advice.

2. Let other members talk without interruption.

3. Everyone should try to share in the group, but no one should monopolize the group's time.

4. Be interested in what someone else shares. Listen with your heart. Never converse privately with someone while another person is talking. Never belittle another's beliefs or expressions.

5. Be committed to express your feelings from your heart.

6. Help others own their feelings and take responsibility for change in their lives. Don't jump in with easy answers or a story on how you conquered the same problem or automatically give a scripture as a "pat answer." Relate to where they are.

7. Avoid accusing or blaming. Speak in the "I" mode about how something or someone made you feel. Example: "I felt angry when. . . ."

8. Avoid ill-timed humor to lighten emotionally-charged times. Let participants work through their sharing even if it is hard.

9. Keep names and sharing of other group members CONFIDENTIAL.

10. Because we are all in various stages of growth, please give others permission to be where they are in their growth. Support group is a "safe place" for all to grow and share their lives.

11. Make an effort to prepare your homework for each session.

12. Pray for other group members and enjoy the new relationships.

Leaders will be first and foremost responsible for

modeling and upholding these guidelines for the group. When leaders model these guidelines, the group will be operating on a strong foundation.

A WORD ABOUT CONFIDENTIALITY

Because of its importance, *confidentiality* deserves special emphasis.

Aglow support groups are called "safe places." Part of what makes them safe is that nothing shared within the group ever goes outside the group. The assurance of confidentiality enables group members to become open, honest, transparent, vulnerable, and trusting.

Leaders and group members MUST NOT share:

1. Names of those attending the group.
2. Anything spoken or shared within the group.

The group leader must stress the importance of everything remaining confidential and she must be willing to confront when it is violated. Members are to know that they are not to share what others disclose in the group with mates, friends, pastors, Aglow boards, or any other person.

Confidentiality is an expression of love, respect, and maturity.

WORK AND RESPONSIBILITY

This look into support groups has revealed the characteristics that distinguish them from other groups. It is good to see how the dynamics of support groups enable them to fulfill the purposes of this type of ministry. These features are distinct and must be used for the groups to succeed.

You will find as you train to be a support group leader, there is real work and responsibility involved in this privilege.

The next chapter provides you with an understanding of the organizational process, thus making a support group more manageable.

15

...

Outlines and Formats

God is a God of order. We see it from His first move as Creator when He brought order out of chaos. Created in His image, we too function best when there is a plan and order to what we are doing. This chapter gives order to the support group process through formats, outlines, and check lists. These *helps* will be on separate pages so that you may duplicate them and use them as needed.

Now we are going to have a walk-through in order to check out each leader's responsibilities and the meeting format. Our goal is to see that all is in order and we are ready for the support group to begin. Please note that Aglow does not require support group leaders to use these lists. They are available to use at your option.

Get your clipboards ready and follow me.

AGLOW SUPPORT GROUP WEEKLY
PREPARATION LIST

One week before your group meets:

___ 1. Prepare the material, work through discussion questions.

___ 2. Talk to co-leader about plans, and/or delegate.

___ 3. Assemble any materials needed for group.

___ 4. Pray for group members and group.

Three days before:

___ 1. Confirm meeting place (If you have an Aglow group hostess, check in with her on details: seating, snacks, etc. (See *Leader's Digest*, Section 8, p. 135).

___ 2. Call those who missed last week.

___ 3. Review material and go over leadership skills.

___ 4. Confer with co-leader on materials and preparations.

___ 5. Pray with co-leader for group.

Day of meeting:

___ 1. Review leadership skills and material.

___ 2. Pray.

___ 3. Deal with any last minute details.

___ 4. Arrive early.

___ 5. Check room or with hostess for lights, seating, temperature, etc. Create a comfortable atmosphere.

___ 6. Pray with co-leader before others arrive.

___ 7. Warmly welcome group members.

AGLOW SUPPORT GROUP MEETING OUTLINE*

Always begin on time.

Note: The number of minutes to the right of each section is a guide to what is appropriate. The leader will be responsible to watch the time and move the group on to the next section. This is an area of discipline that the group will learn to appreciate and cooperate with. As leader you will learn to proportion the time as you prepare for the session.

OPENING   (10-15 min.)

A. Word of welcome. Leaders introduce themselves.

B. Prayer and/or one song. Group member may lead.

C. Offering (optional)

D. Read Guidelines
   1. Include at each meeting
   2. Reinforces concepts if group members read
   3. Helps members feel comfortable sharing in a group

E. Introductions
   1. May prefer first names only
   2. Do first 2 or 3 sessions
   3. Do when new people come

FACILITATING

A. Follow-up   (5-15 min.)
   Feedback from group on how they applied last session in their lives and/or questions

B. Review of New Material (10-20 min.)
   1. Avoid teaching too much.
   2. Have group share what's in material.

C. Group Discussion (30-45 min.)

CLOSING (5-15 min.)   (Close on time)

A. Summary
   1. Leader or group member "sums-up" the discussion time by sharing what was heard.
   2. Leader can emphasize truth and correct wrong concepts.
   3. Leader exhorts group to trust in God and His process of change and goal of the group.
   4. Leader should always end group by giving hope and expressing love.

B. Assignments
Explain any homework assignments.

C. Prayer
   1. Always express hope and faith.
   2. May be done by group member.

D. Ministry
Offer ministry to those who feel need.

AGLOW SUPPORT GROUP SESSION ASSESSMENT

Using this list after each session will help you see areas that need work and areas that are working well. You may want your co-leader to do one separately and then compare answers or you may want to go over it together. It is best to complete it within 24 hours of the session while things are fresh in your mind.

You are not being graded, so view this evaluation as a helping tool to becoming an effective leader and having a successful group.

A simple *yes* or *no* before each question is enough evaluation.

         1. Began and ended on time.
         2. Group felt welcome and loved.
         3. Members had prepared their homework.
         4. Teaching was stimulating and not preachy.
         5. Members are not cliquish.
         6. Most shared freely.
         7. Group honored guidelines.
         8. Discussion flowed well.
         9. Growth can be seen in members.
         10. Members are caring toward one another.
         11. Leader was listening effectively.
         12. Leader was effective with questions.
         13. Leader kept group focused on godly change.
         14. Conflict was handled effectively.
         15. Members left feeling encouraged and hopeful.

Areas that are working well: _____
_____
_____
_____
_____

Areas that need attention:_____

_____

_____

_____

_____

Specific things we can do to solve any problems: _____

_____

_____

_____

_____

_____

_____

This form can assist you in praying effectively for your group and for yourself and your co-leader.

AGLOW SUPPORT GROUP LEADER'S PERSONAL ASSESSMENT

This is adapted from Rapha's *Right Step Facilitator Training Manual*:

1. Am I humble?

And He sat down, called the twelve and said to them, "If anyone desires to be first, he shall be last of all, and servant of all" (Mark 9:35).

2. Do I minister with boldness?

According to my earnest expectation and hope that in nothing I shall be ashamed, but that with all boldness, as always, so now also Christ will be magnified in my body, whether by life or by death (Phil. 1:20).

3. Does my attitude reflect the joy of the Lord?

"These things I have spoken to you, that My joy may remain in you, and that your joy may be full" (John 15:11).

4. Am I able to love?

"The second is like it, 'You shall love your neighbor as yourself'" (Matt. 22:39).

5. Am I listening and obedient to God's direction?

But God has revealed them to us through His Spirit. For the Spirit searches all things, yes, the deep things of God (1 Cor. 2:10).

6. Do I maintain confidentiality?

A perverse man stirs up dissension, and a gossip separates close friends (Prov.16:28 NIV).

7. Am I submitting to the leadership I am placed under in this ministry? Am I really a servant to Christ, or do I have my own agenda?

Slaves, be obedient to those who are your masters according to the flesh, with fear and trembling, in sincerity of heart, as to Christ" (Eph. 6:5).[1]

PRAYER PRIORITY

Please note that prayer is a consistent element on the preparation check list and in the meeting outline. God alone is the source of life, change, mercy, grace, and love for our groups. He alone has the wisdom and guidance you need as you work with His precious possessions, His people.

The more constant you are in prayer and the more reliant you are on Him, the more effective your group will be and the more fulfilled you will be.

Leading a group requires great giving of self, but the self you are to give is the self that is continually being filled with His Spirit, for His service. And isn't it good news that God doesn't expect us to do it ourselves, but He delights in coming along side as Helper, Enabler, and Friend?

SUMMARY

This section has given you a look inside support groups in order to appreciate their uniqueness and give you ways to organize and evaluate your groups. You are beginning to get a picture of what a support group is like, but you may not be able to see yourself in that picture yet.

Section Five, KNOW YOUR SKILLS, will define and explain the skills you will use as group leader; hopefully, you will begin to see yourself as the leader in that group you picture.

You have now completed the reading in Section Four. Please turn to the worksheets for this section on page 219, and reproduce a copy. Then fill in your answers on the copy. If you are applying to become an Aglow support group leader, mail your completed sheets to Jennie Newbrough at the address on page 202. Be sure to include a stamped, self-addressed, business size (#10) envelope to facilitate their return. If you are reading for your own edification, you also may want to reproduce the worksheets, fill them in, and keep them as part of your self-study.

Section V

Know Your Skills

THE PRIVILEGE of this section is to discover the skills that will enable you to be an effective support group leader.

THE CHALLENGE of this section is to make these skills your own and let them come to life as you lead a support group.

16
...

A Right Foundation

"Overnight Success." "Immediate Results." "Instant Action." Headlines such as these catch my attention. "Now" has such a tremendous appeal to me, much more than "Work in Progress" or "Job Under Construction." I'm sure I'm not alone in wrestling with that time gap between when I want something to happen and the moment it does. For people accustomed to fast action, waiting can feel like sitting out a life sentence.

Thank goodness, God sees the bigger picture. He moves freely through time and eternity, on schedule and on course in His divine love and perspective. When He calls us to serve Him, He graciously overrides our impatience to move ahead by challenging us to become equipped and prepared for the tasks ahead. In fact, He never calls us without equipping us. Yet to our surprise, such preparation often requires much time and diligent effort.

It would be nice if you awakened tomorrow morning filled with all the skill and ability to be the very best support group leader you could be. But this is the real world and God requires real commitment from us and this involves our willingness to work at acquiring ministry skills—a test of our commitment and dependability.

EQUIPPING, THE BIBLICAL VIEW

Paul instructed Timothy:

Do your best to present yourself to God as one approved, a workman who does not need to be ashamed and who correctly handles the word of truth (2 Tim. 2:15 NIV).

and:

Be diligent in these matters; give yourself wholly to them, so that everyone may see your progress (1 Tim. 4:15).

David was only a young zealous shepherd boy when God called him to lead the entire nation of Israel. Was God crazy?

No. He didn't look at outward appearances; He saw the heartbeat of a man who would serve Him well and He enlisted him for the Kingdom. Nevertheless, He still required this young shepherd boy to enter the "school of the cave." Here, avoiding the spears of Saul, David learned the wisdom and ways of God. And the results? Listen to the psalmist's words:

He chose David his servant and took him from the sheep pens; from tending the sheep he brought him to be the shepherd of his people Jacob, of Israel his inheritance, And David shepherded them with integrity of heart; with skillful hands he led them (Ps. 78:70-72 NIV).

It is this integrity of heart and skillfulness that we aspire to as Aglow support group leaders.

PRACTICING THE SKILLS

In Section Five, we explore the various skills used in leading support groups. Just reading about skills, however, will not produce skillfulness. You will become skillful as you WORK with them.

I recommend that you practice these new skills in conversations with family, friends, and anywhere else you can. You can tell them that you are working on these skills and ask their cooperation or you can simply just be quietly aware of what you are doing as you use them.

If you watch any talk shows on television, you can also practice by interacting with what is taking place on the show. Think of what you would ask or say to the people sharing their lives.

USING PRAYER AND PRACTICE

When you actually begin leading a support group, you will use prayer and practice to work the skills. I encourage you to pray for the Holy Spirit's help with specific skills and then to concentrate on deliberately using each skill. After a few weeks you will be using all of the skills quite naturally. You'll be delighted when you hear yourself clarifying or expounding without deliberate thought.

SKILLS OF THE HEART

The most important element in support group leadership is the *quality* of your presence. Your presence must convey genuine love, concern, and desire to help. When what you give is not genuine, the others will know it.

If the group members are to risk opening their hearts and being vulnerable, an attitude of trust must be established. The members will need to trust you before they can trust others in the group. That's where trust begins—with the leader. If your presence is not genuine, this trust will never be established. Your honest care and godly love— the skills of the heart—are the foundational skills that all other skills build upon.

Other sections of this guide have given you opportunity to determine if this is the time for you to lead a group. Our reference to a genuine heart is to reaffirm this essential motive and to encourage you to prepare your heart before each support group session.

Some days you may not feel fully present for the group. When this happens, pray and seek to release yourself from everything that distracts. If you still feel distracted, let the group know so the women won't take it personally.

Say something such as, "This has been an intense day for me. If I seem 'not all here' please forgive me." This is a time when a co-leader is a really special asset to both you and the group.

THE RIGHT FOUNDATION

The skills of the heart become the right foundation upon which we build an effective support group ministry. With these in hand, the group can come to life with form and function as we apply our other support skills.

We place these skills in two basic categories: *attending* and *probing*. The following two chapters will define and develop these skills and prepare you to use them as a support group leader.

17

· · ·

Attending Skills

In this chapter we will look at several dimensions of what we call *attending* a support group.

Attending means giving your full attention to the person or task at hand. As a support group leader, you are "fully present" for each person when she shares and for the group as a whole as they listen and respond. It isn't always easy to be "fully present," but it is the stance you need as leader.

While this may be a new concept for many, it is one which is easily understood. In the general sense, attending a group includes what you give of yourself and what you draw from the group.

You will soon discover, as a support group leader, that you get what you give. If you listen intently to group members, they will share more deeply; if you observe more closely, you will see more keenly.

Attending the group involves:

1. Observing each person as she shares
2. Observing the group as they listen
3. Responding appropriately to the one sharing

4. Responding to the group
5. Maintaining group guidelines
6. Keeping the group focused
7. Conveying love and truth

Sounds like a juggling act, doesn't it? If you've always wanted to learn to juggle, this is your chance! Joking aside, you can see that attending is a skill with many challenges. Just like the juggler who learned to keep three oranges in the air at once by handling one at a time first, so you can learn one concept at a time.

LISTENING

Listening is the primary attending skill, and it has two dimensions: How you listen. What you hear.

How You Listen

This aspect of attending focuses on you, the leader, what you give, and what your presence conveys to the group, including your body language, and your voice. Some body language suggestions for reinforcing how well you listen are

- Fully face the person speaking.
- Make eye contact.
- Lean in to encourage them to continue at appropriate times.
- Maintain an "open posture" such as arms resting easily on your lap.

Avoid:

- Looking away
- Fidgeting or playing with something
- "Closed" gestures, such as folding your arms
- Posture that suggests disinterest, such as sitting sideways or slouching

Some voice suggestions to accentuate how well you listen are:

- Use voice softness to be friendly, gentle, caring.
- Watch tone of voice and rate of speech.
- Use recognizing sounds to show you are with them, e.g., "Yes," "Uh-huh" "Oh," "Hmmmm."

Avoid:

- Ill-timed humor
- Parental words and/or tone
- Vocabulary that is below/above group
- Sighs which may signal boredom

Your full attention gives a message of encouragement, acceptance, and significance to the members of the group. To turn from the group means to avert. If your body language, voice, or countenance is averted the group may feel your heart is also averted. It is important to be aware of what you are conveying to them, as well as what they are conveying to you. A group leader must be self-controlled, self-aware, and others-centered.

What You Hear

This element of attending focuses on the group members, what they share, and how they share it.

Your goal is to listen to the whole person. You will hear both verbal and non-verbal messages. You will be listening to hear the inner person as well as the outer person. Non-verbal messages include

- Body language, posture.
- Facial expression.
- Body movement—fidgeting, playing with things may indicate anxiety.
- "Attitude" i.e. aloofness may indicate fear or anger.

- Grooming—may indicate self-worth or depression.
- Conflicting messages—the person says she is fine, but her facial expression and grooming denote depression; person says she loves her mate, but arms are crossed and hands clinched, denoting tension or anger.

Non-verbal messages are clues as to what is going on inside that the person herself may not be aware of. These clues give you direction in asking questions, but it is best to avoid commenting directly on the body language.

For instance, you would not want to say, "I've noticed by your unkempt clothing that you may be depressed." However, you could ask, "What feelings or thoughts of discouragement or unhappiness are you having?" Direct comments on body language usually make everyone feel self-conscious and thereby stifle the person or group. It is important to be sensitive to each person's feelings, aiming for an atmosphere in which people feel free to be just who they are.

Verbal messages include:

- Words—the words people use are their most direct way of saying what they think and feel. Listen to their choice of words and the thoughts they are expressing. These give clues as to where they are educationally, socially, or emotionally. A person who uses technical terms and intellect may actually "be there" or she may be using language to distance herself and thereby hide from her feelings. A person who says, "Oh, I'm dumb. I don't know how to talk," may indeed be lacking or she may be expressing low self-worth or avoiding responsibility. As with non-verbal messages, there are specific clues:
- Tone of voice—a loud or shrill tone may indicate a need to be noticed, a desire to control, or anxiety. A low soft voice may indicate timidity, low self-worth, or subtle control. Tone of voice should be appropriate for what the person is sharing. Anger is more forceful than joy.

• Rate of speech—slow, drawn-out speech may be timidity, control, vagueness, self-consciousness. Rapid speech may be nervousness, control, insecurity, need for attention, or enthusiasm.

• Attitude—a person's general attitude toward the subject she is discussing, the group, the leader, life, God, etc., will be conveyed with her verbal communication. These attitudes include: cynicism, joy, criticism, acceptance. All are significant clues to the inner person.

• Missing pieces—often people will avoid the issues they most need to talk about. If someone talks about all her family, but never mentions her father, then this "missing piece" may be the most important part. Once again, this is a clue to you. You could ask, "What can you share with us about your father?"

All messages, verbal and non-verbal, should be appropriate to what is being shared and should change with subjects and situations. If there are extremes, such as someone who is always very joyful or always very angry or always non-expressive, these may be signs that the person has some deep issues. These issues may either be exposed and resolved as the group develops or handled by referring the person to a counselor or a doctor.

The goal of *attending* is to invest yourself in such a way that the group members become comfortable being open so that you can truly see them and help them see themselves.

BLOCKS TO AVOID

Road signs give wonderful safety tips for drivers. It's a lot easier to avoid going too fast on a sharp turn or to swerve past a chuck hole if you know about them ahead of time. In the same way, there are some blocks that you should know about ahead of time as you *attend* your group, blocks that will greatly hinder openness and communication. As the leader, you should avoid these blocks yourself as well as caution the group against using them. We have listed eight blocks:

1. *Moralizing*—"You should, shouldn't, ought, must." These parental terms imply guilt, shame, blame. The feeling they give is that you are above, looking down at the other person with judgment.

2. *Advising*—"This is what you need to do." "This is what I did." "What I would do is. . . ." As group leaders we are not trying to "fix" others. *We do not give directive advice.* Remember, you are not the one to go home and live out this advice, nor will you be affected by its consequences. What may be healthy or appropriate in one situation may not be in this one. You only see the part of the picture the group member shares with you.

What you can do when someone asks, "What do you think I should do?" is turn the question back and say, "Let's talk about your options. What choices do you think there are in your situation?" As you discuss options, help her look at the benefits as well as the difficulties that may result from each option. She doesn't have to make a decision right away.

Just knowing she has choices to consider can be very freeing. I encourage people to choose the options they are best prepared to live with at this time.

3. *Sympathizing*—"Don't worry. Everything will be okay" or "Oh, that's just horrible!" This type of response either invalidates a person's feelings or gives her no hope. Empathy feels with the person, e.g., "This is really difficult for you." The person feels supported and validated.

4. *Lecturing, teaching, preaching*—These are also parental responses that talk down to the person. You are not their superior, but their friend. You are not to discipline, but to support. Rather than lecture, ask, "What do you think you are learning from this experience?" or "What is the Lord showing you?"

5. *Withdrawing*—To withdraw means to pull back from. Comments such as, "Oh, that's nothing to worry about," may be well-intentioned, but it gives the message that the person's sharing is not important. Certain actions also give

that same message: looking around while a person is sharing, moving to another person, or changing the subject without acknowledging the person sharing invalidates the person or the person's thoughts or feelings.

We withdraw when we are uninterested or unconcerned. Avoid giving this message.

6. *Inappropriate humor*—Appropriate humor can lighten the group, but avoid humorous comments when a person has shared a situation or feeling that is personal or significant for her. Ill-timed or misused humor is abusive.

Avoid nervous humor. Often when a sensitive subject is discussed, there are those who have a nervous response of humor or laughter. If this happens in the group, do not join in the laughter, but remain focused on the person who is sharing and continue to validate her with your attention. This will bring the group back to focus and minimize the effect of the laughter.

7. *Bias*—We all have biases or preferences of thinking. In some instances they may have become a harmful form of prejudice. It is important to be aware of your own biases, but you must discipline yourself to refrain from letting them interfere with your acceptance of those in the group.

As a Christian counselor I counsel those from just about every denomination, even though I am not in agreement with all the various denominational teachings. I limit my counsel and comments to the Word of God and avoid areas of difference that are not significant to our purpose.

8. *Selective listening*—This means hearing or only listening to what we want to hear. Usually, we will not really "hear" the heart of the other person when we listen this way. For example:

"I was very hurt when I lost my job."

Selective listener: "What kind of a job did you have?"

The most important issue shared is that the person who lost her job is hurt; what type of job is a secondary issue.

EMOTIONS

A challenge that always arises with *attending* is how emotions are handled, the group's and our own. Emotions are a God-given part of our soul that should be respected. Some people are very emotional. Others have no idea what they feel; their feelings are "frozen." As the leader, you will need to encourage the emotional ones to keep their emotions in balance and the frozen ones to get in touch with what they feel.

The Lord wants us in touch with our feelings. Feelings are an indication of what we are experiencing. We are to be in touch with our feelings. In a pictorial sense, we are to hold them "with our finger tips," but we should not hold on to them or grasp them in our fists or they may grab hold of us and we will be controlled by them.

An emotional person can be guided into balance by gently talking her through the emotion and into thinking. Let me illustrate with a woman experiencing widowhood:

Sally: "I can't bear to live without my husband." (She is sobbing as she tells this to the group.)

Leader: "It is very hard, Sally. You were married a long time. You had many plans for the future together. What were some of those plans?"

Sally: Shares some of the plans.

Leader: "If he were here, would Joe be happy if you completed any of those plans?"

Sally: Is now thinking ahead as well as feeling the moment.

Because support group is a safe place, it is a good place to express feelings. Anger, fear, grief may all be expressed in various intensities at times. Allow space for these emotions to be released. Some group members may be uncomfortable, but reassure the group that the release is good.

A person with frozen feelings will often "thaw" in a

group; as others express feelings, she begins to recognize her own. Encourage her when you see this happening.

We do not want emotions *ruling* the group time, but we do want to allow time for release and response. Response is what guides the feeling. When a person has had a significant emotional release, give her time to compose herself, then ask if she can share what her thoughts or feelings are about the release.

For example: One woman might say, "Now that I've said how much I hate him, I realize I don't hate him. I'm just so hurt that he doesn't seem to care." This response to the release reveals a purpose for the release and guides the emotion in a productive direction. She may also be open to some group response at this time.

The key to handling emotions in a group is to guide, not control.

SILENCE

Silence may occur at times in your group. Its presence does not mean you are ineffective. Actually it is a very effective support group dynamic.

When silence occurs, pray quietly for the Lord to work. Silence provides:

- Time for personal reflection
- Time to absorb and integrate
- Time for you to observe
- Time to switch direction

Silence is intimate. Let the group savor it. Usually someone will break the silence; if not, you may when you feel a release from the Lord. You can simply say, "It was good to be still before the Lord." You might then ask if anyone has anything to share. The Lord wants to be part of our group and this may have been His sharing time.

Let silence do its work.

SUMMARY

Attending is being fully present for the group. This chapter has explored attending skills that will enable you to be effectively present for your group.

Now that you have a sense of being present and hearing your group, you are ready for the probing skills in Chapter 18 that will bring the group to life.

It is challenging to juggle all of these skills, but take heart:

The hearing ear and the seeing eye,
The Lord has made both of them (Prov. 20:12).

18

...

Probing Skills

This chapter may be the one you've been waiting for since you first picked up this guide. Here we take a close look at the *probing skills*, the actual skills you will use to cause the support group to function.

Probing skills include the way you ask questions or give comments in order to (1) help group members share and (2) promote interaction in the group. Like any other skill, asking good questions takes learning and practice. You will need to know:

WHAT questions to ask
WHEN to ask them
HOW to ask them

THE PURPOSE OF PROBING

Actually, probing skills are not just questions but comments and statements that enable the group members to see more clearly who they are and what they are experiencing. When a painting is being restored, delicate chemicals are used to remove layers until the fine original work of art is displayed. This is how I like to think of probing skills—as those delicate elements that are applied until the truth is revealed.

The purpose of probing is

1. To enter into the world of group members
2. To gather information
3. To give information
4. To help members take more effective control of their lives

When a skillful, probing question and/or comment is made, a group member has the opportunity to reflect and answer personally where she is. This reflection helps her on her way to self-discovery and self-responsibility, two of the main goals of support groups.

Dr. Gerald Corey, in his book *Theory and Practice of Group Counseling* says: "Skillfully executed questions help members focus on what they are doing, what they are thinking, and how they are feeling."[1] The following are sample questions from Dr. Corey's book:

"You say you would like to be more active in your classes. How many times did you participate in discussions this past week?"

"You say you would like to have more fun in your life. What have you done in the past few days that you consider to be fun?"

"Describe a time when you felt self-confident. What were you doing?"

"What are some of the best (or worst) things that would happen if you were to change?"

"What steps toward change could you make right now?"[2]

These comments and questions draw the person out, lift her up, and enable her to see within.[2]

TYPES OF QUESTIONS

In *Rapha's Handbook for Group Leaders*, there is a very strong statement about questions which, in my opinion, every support group leader needs to remember. It is this: "Your group discussions live and die based upon the questions you ask."[3] Indeed, probing skills are the heartbeat of a support group.

The following questions, adapted from Rapha's handbook, provide five examples of different types of questions you might use as support group leader:

1. *Leading* :   Yes or no answer needed
   Expects agreement
   Answer is implied in the question
   Is directive and should be used
      infrequently

   Example   "You do know what the Bible says the
      Kingdom of God is, don't you?"

2. *Limiting:*   Expects a specific answer
   Quiz-like
   Can make people uncomfortable
   Can help promote thinking, participation,
      and expounding on truth
   Use cautiously

   Example: "What three things does the Bible say the
      Kingdom of God is?"

3. *Open:*   Ask who, what, when, where, how, and
      why
   Answer does not limit input
   Welcomes thoughts and feelings
   Very effective
   Use often

   Example: "How do you see righteousness, peace,
      and joy as the Kingdom of God?"

4. *Return:*   When a group member asks you a question, you may turn it back to her

Keeps the group from focusing on you encourages self-discovery

Example: "*I* would like to know how *you* see joy as the Kingdom of God in your life."

5. *Relay:*   When a question is directed to you, extend it to the group

Promotes interaction

Is constructive

Example: "Peace for me means I've relinquished control to God. What does it mean to the rest of you?"

OTHER PROBING SKILLS

In addition to questions, the following four probing skills are used often:

1. Restating or Rephrasing

To paraphrase back what you thought was said "I hear you saying you felt. . . ."

2. Clarifying

To make sure you hear correctly, ask group members to explain further. "I'm not sure I'm hearing what you meant when you said. . . ."

3. Extending

Encourage members to be more specific or continue sharing. "Can you give me an example?"

4. Giving Feedback

To make a response to what has been shared. This is best done with permission. "Could I give some input to what I've heard?" or "Are you open to hearing feedback on that?"

SUPPORT GROUP SKILLS AND DYNAMICS

The following chart will be an invaluable tool for ready reference. It lists all the support group skills and dynamics.

Skills	Description	Aims and Desired Outcomes
Active listening	Attending to verbal and nonverbal aspects of communication without judging or evaluating	To encourage trust and [participant] self-disclosure and exploration.
Restating	Saying in slightly different words what a participant has said to clarify its meaning.	To determine if the leader has understood correctly the participant's statement; to provide support and clarification.
Clarifying	Grasping the essence of a message at both the feeling and the thinking levels; simplifying [participant] statements by focusing on the core of the message.	To help participants sort out conflicting and confused feelings and thoughts; to arrive at a meaningful understanding of what is being communicated.
Summarizing	Pulling together the important elements of an interaction or session.	To avoid fragmentation and give direction to a session; to provide for continuity and meaning.
Questioning	Asking open-ended questions that lead to self-exploration of the "what" and "how" of behavior.	To elicit further discussion; to get information; to stimulate thinking; to increase clarity and focus; to provide for further self-exploration.
Interpreting	Offering possible explanations for certain behaviors, feelings, and thoughts.	To encourage deeper self-exploration; to provide a new perspective for considering and understanding one's behavior.

Skills	Description	Aims and Desired Outcomes
Confronting	Challenging participants to look at discrepancies between their words and actions or body and verbal messages; pointing to conflicting information or messages.	To encourage honest self-investigation; to provide a new perspective for considering and understanding one's behavior.
Reflecting feelings	Communicating understanding of the content of feelings.	To let participants know that they are heard and understood beyond the level of words.
Supporting	Providing encouragement and reinforcement.	To create an atmosphere that encourages participants to continue desired behaviors; to provide help when [participants] are facing difficult struggles; to create trust.
Empathizing	Identifying with [participants] by assuming their frames of reference.	To foster trust in the therapeutic relationship; to communicate understanding; to encourage deeper levels of self-exploration.
Facilitating	Opening up clear and direct communication within the group, helping participants assume increasing responsibility for the group's direction.	To promote effective communication among participants; to help participants reach their own goals in the group.
Initiating	Promoting group participation and introducing new directions in the group.	To prevent needless group floundering; to increase the pace of group process.

SKILLS	DESCRIPTION	AIMS AND DESIRED OUTCOMES
Goal setting	Planning specific goals for the group process and helping participants define concrete and meaningful goals.	To give direction to the group's activities; to help members select and clarify their goals.
Evaluating	Appraising the ongoing group process and the individual and group dynamics.	To promote better self-awareness and understanding of group movement and direction.
Giving feedback	Expressing concrete and honest reactions based on observation of participants' behaviors.	To offer an external view of how the person appears to others; to increase the [participant's] self-awareness.
Protecting	Safeguarding participants from unnecessary psychological risks in the group.	To warn participants of possible risks in group participation; to reduce these risks.
Disclosing oneself	Revealing one's reactions to here-and-now events in the group.	To facilitate deeper levels of group interaction; to create trust; to model ways of revealing oneself to others.
Modeling	Demonstrating desired behavior through actions.	To provide examples of desirable behavior; to inspire participants to fully develop their potential.
Linking	Connecting the work that participants do to common themes in the group.	To promote participant-to-participant interactions; to encourage the development of cohesion.

Skills	Description	Aims and Desired Outcomes
Blocking	Intervening to stop counterproductive group behavior.	To protect participants; to enhance the flow of group process.
Terminating	Preparing the group to close a session or end its existence.	To help participants assimilate, integrate, and apply in-group learning to everyday life.[4]

WORDS OF CAUTION AND ENCOURAGEMENT

Most of us can recall taking a class and being so excited by what we were learning, we wanted to share our information with everyone we saw. Whether it was a college psychology class or a class on bread making, sometimes, in our zeal with a new challenge, we "overdid" our expertise. The same can happen with probing skills. Let me give you a word of caution: Do not overuse them.

It is not necessary to comment back to every person or to comment on every thing a person says. Be sensitive. Develop wisdom as to when to use probing. Overuse will hinder the group. The last thing you want is for anyone to feel she is on trial!

When the group begins, you will be modeling the skills, but as the group develops, let the women adapt the skills. Eventually they should be doing most of the probing with one another. An effective support group leader gives her skills away and begins to diminish in prominence. When that happens, you have a support group.

Of course you will need practice and prayer to become adept at all these skills. But be encouraged. They really are much more natural than you may think and the Lord will be very much with you. After all, that is what is on His heart—the Body of Christ ministering one to another.

FACILITATING GOALS

Do you remember that we started this guide talking about a journey—a journey to discover support group ministry? In a real sense, you as a leader will be on that same journey. One of your destinations will be to achieve the goal of open and responsible communication.

Corey and Corey in their book *Groups: Process and Practice*, list seven facilitating goals that will help you reach that destination. They are

1. Assist members to express honestly their fears and expectations.
2. Work to create an atmosphere of safety and acceptance.
3. Encourage and support members as they explore new ideas and behaviors.
4. Involve as many people as possible in the interaction.
5. Work to lessen dependency upon the group leader.
6. Encourage open expression of conflict and controversy.
7. Help members remove hindrances to direct communication.[5]

THE HOLY SPIRIT'S HELP

Jesus was a very good communicator. In His time at the well with the Samaritan woman He used many probing and attending skills. Look at this interaction in John 4 and see how He used questions and "clues" that she gave Him. These clues gave her insight and opened her to hearing the truth. He used a word in each of her comments to lead her into truth.

As Christians we know He used the insight of the Holy Spirit, not "skills" per se. We use this same insight through the gifts of the Holy Spirit. This is why it is so important to pray before, during, and after group. The gifts of knowledge, wisdom, and discerning of spirits will guide you in asking questions and attending the group.

You are challenged to learn and apply the skills in this text.

You are challenged to minister the fruits of the Holy Spirit.

You are challenged to have the heart of God for His people.

You are privileged to be enabled by the Holy Spirit.

19
...
Possible Problems

Getting along. That's easy. Easy, that is, if there aren't any people involved. We smile in knowing agreement at this familiar adage because we know what human beings are like. We know that when people gather together they don't come alone. They come carrying their own "baggage" with them, their own sets of emotions, problems, and difficulties. That's exactly how they'll be coming to your support group.

Unfortunately, "baggage" gets heavy, both for the ones carrying it and for the ones who bump into it. Meeting hurt feelings and defensiveness can be like barking your shins against a metal footlocker. Hurt people *hurt people*.

You will need to be prepared because difficult situations inevitably arise in the groups, but handled well, they can contribute to the healing process and prove to be exciting opportunities for growth.

The most important truth to remember is: people are not the problem, it's their behavior. And most often, people are not aware of their behavior or the problems it presents.

This guide has consistently presented God's heart for

His people as the most important element of support group leadership, and this heart of compassion and supportive love is most essential in handling these problems and the people who present them.

In Christ Jesus there is no condemnation. Neither is there criticism, judgment, or impatience.

DEAL WITH YOUR OWN WEAKNESSES

Being in a support group in many ways is like being in a room filled with mirrors. You will see yourself more clearly as you are confronted with others' problems. You will become aware of areas of weakness in your own soul. This is a healthy and positive dynamic and a way the Holy Spirit can help us, leaders included. If you are controlling, impatient, or insecure, group problems will touch those areas in you. That is why the first place you, as the leader, deal with the problem and the person is with God. Go to Him in prayer and ask for His heart for that person. Ask for insight into why she is doing what she does and ask for God's gentle spirit in dealing with her.

Confronting in love is mature and necessary. If confrontation is difficult for you, be aware that you will have to deal with the problem eventually. Putting it off will only give room for it to grow and spread into the group. If you delay, a group member may take control and produce another problem. The group will respect you for addressing the problems in love.

Remember, too, that the guidelines exist for a purpose. The first line of defense for any problem is to remind the group of the guidelines. If the guidelines are read at each meeting, the person presenting the problem may see herself and choose to change without a word from you.

HELPS FOR POTENTIAL PROBLEMS

Listed below are potential problems and suggested ways of dealing with them:

The Talker

This person has a great need to express herself verbally. She may be nervous, fearful, controlling, or very needy. Most talkers are not deliberately selfish, but they can put a real strain on the group.

Your Action:

Go ahead and interrupt in a gentle way. "Ann, you have shared a lot and I would like to ask the group if they identify or have a response." If gentle comments don't convey the message and excessive talking is a consistent problem, talk with the person privately after a group session. She may need to be told directly what she is doing. Be her friend and tell her you want to help her with this. Perhaps having some private time with you to tell "the whole story" will help. Reassure her that you want her to share but within the limits of the guidelines. If this still doesn't help, you may just have to be very open in the group and tell her that her time is up.

The Silent One

The withdrawn, quiet group member may be shy, fearful, insecure, or resistant; but it is important to draw her into the group.

Your Action:

Without pressure, consistently ask for comments from her. Having her read the guidelines or a scripture may help her feel comfortable speaking in the group. Acknowledge her presence before group time, letting her know you are glad she is there. Privately you may ask if you could make it easier for her in any way or if there is a problem.

The Dominator

This person always has a comment, has a hard time with silence, will step in and lead if she can. She may be controlling or just very enthusiastic. She has a need to be needed or be noticed.

Your Action:

Sometimes giving her a responsibility can help. Telling her beforehand that you would like her to summarize at the end and to hold her comments until then can give direction and purpose. It is essential that you be a firm leader and deal with this as soon as it begins. Be sensitive. Dominators are usually not as self-confident as they appear and will feel rejection easily. A private talk will probably be helpful.

The Fixer

Most groups will have someone who wants to give advice and rescue. Generally this person wants to give solutions to everyone's problems.

Your Action:

Reinforce the guidelines. Express appreciation for her desire to help, but gently point out she is trying to rescue.

The Contender

This person usually has a root of anger and is resistant to input. She tends to argue easily and can bring a lot of tension into the group.

Your Action:

Let her express anger that is not directed at someone in the group. She needs a release. Interrupt if she is hostile to group members. Let her know this will not be tolerated. If she is argumentative, ask her to stop. Do not recognize her input, but move on. A private discussion may be helpful.

The Wanderer

Someone may begin discussing an idea that is off track and the group will follow that subject.

Your Action:

Gently remind the group of your topic and ask a question to bring the group back to focus.

HANDLE WITH CARE

There may be other problems that arise in a group and

they should be handled in the same loving, caring way. Be gentle, friendly, light-hearted. No one has committed a crime; people are just learning to relate. If you have a tendency to control, you will really have to discipline yourself at these times.

As the group matures and has spent some time together, you can let the group "discipline" each other. One way of doing this is by having the other members tell the "offending" member how it affects them when someone dominates or rescues. Often the whole group grows as the women learn to lovingly confront and safely receive. For many, this will be their first experience with healthy "family" interaction. Allow them to learn.

It is important that you not let the threat of potential problems keep you from being willing to minister. We should not let fear cause us to fail to care. The joys you will experience in seeing lives transformed will be far more significant than the problems you will encounter.

Remember, process the problems in prayer.

20

...

His Final Touch

The ribbons of **privilege** and **challenge** have been woven throughout this book.

The strands of challenge have been knitted together to give knowledge and understanding in

- Knowing God
- Knowing yourself
- Knowing people
- Knowing support groups
- Knowing skills

The threads of understanding have been braided with the strands of privilege to fulfill the law of Christ:

- To bear one another's burdens
- To be supporting ligaments in the Body of Christ.

We extend these ribbons to you, with prayer that as you tie them securely to your heart you will be strengthened by the Holy Spirit as you hear the Lord say, "Send out laborers into the harvest."

God seldom calls experts. Instead He calls those who are willing to learn, willing to follow, and willing to love.

Prayer and preparation will be the friends that encourage you. Experience will bring you confidence, and love will make it live.

The challenge presented in this text can seem overwhelming. You may feel like that juggler trying to keep all those oranges in the air. Don't despair if you drop a few, if you have some bad group sessions. The disciples did too.

There have been group leaders who were awkward and really unsure of what they were doing, yet who had successful groups because they loved the group members. "Love will cover a multitude of sins" (1 Pet. 4:8).

Don't strive to be a perfect group leader; there is no such animal. Don't be bound to "do it by the book." This text is a guide, not the law. God will work through you if you *prepare* to the best of your ability, *trust* Him throughout the process, and sincerely *love* your group members.

It is the love of God through you that takes the ribbons in hand and ties that marvelous bow of healing, holiness, and eternal life. It is your joy to behold all of this from the heart of God.

May your blessings overflow as you join with Christ in His ministry—one to another.

You have now completed the reading in Section Five. Please turn to the worksheets for this section on page 224, and reproduce a copy. Then fill in your answers on the copy. If you are applying to become an Aglow support group leader, mail your completed sheets to Jennie Newbrough at the address on page 202. Be sure to include a stamped, self-addressed, business size (#10) envelope to facilitate their return. If you are reading for your own edification, you also may want to reproduce the worksheets, fill them in, and keep them as part of your self-study.

Support Group Leader's Worksheets

HOW TO USE THESE SHEETS

The following worksheets are to evaluate your grasp of the support group thinking that is in each section. Each worksheet is designed to help you become an effective support group leader by stimulating your thinking about the material.

Try to relax and see yourself leading your group, and respond as you would to your group members.

We desire to enable you to lead by giving you this opportunity not only to read the material but to work with it as well. It is our way of coming along side you to give personal training.

We believe in you and are pleased to have this opportunity to help equip you for this work of service to the Lord.

You'll want to photocopy these worksheet pages of the book for easy mailing. I will return them with my comments as soon as possible. Please type your answers or write them as legibly as possible to be sure you are understood and to keep the evaluation process easy for us all. Be assured . . . no pass/fail grades will be given.

Each worksheet is divided into two parts:

Part One has questions that require specific answers from the material you have read. **Part Two** requires you to think with the material and respond much like you would in your own support group.

As soon as you finish reading each section, complete the worksheet and mail it to

> Jennie Newbrough
> Support Group Resource Person
> 3708 Woodlawn Way
> Weirton, WV 26062

Please enclose a stamped, self-addressed, business size (#10) envelope with each worksheet to ease return to you, and don't forget to write your name and address on each sheet.

LEADER'S WORKSHEET
SECTION ONE

To Know God
Chapters 1-4

Your Name _____

Your Address_____

City, State, Zip _____

Telephone: Work (_____)_____ Hours _____

          Home (_____) _____

Aglow Fellowship _____

Section One / PART ONE

The following questions require specific answers from the material in Section One.

1. What is the first challenge for any support group leader? _____

_____

2. What does the name, *Elroi,* tell you about God? _____

_____

3. Life is a series of_____ that people avoid

   because they fear _____.

4. List the three stages of change: _____

_____

_____

5. Name four things that can affect our concept of God:

_____

_____

_____

_____

6. There are more than fifty references to _____
   in the New Testament.

7. Many are ashamed if they need help because they have accepted what deception
   from the enemy? _____

8. _____are support group tools
   that challenge us to think and discover truth.

9. What scripture do we call "God's Self-portrait?" _____

_____

10. Which scripture (in NIV) encourages us to "support" one another?

_____

Section One / PART TWO

The following are thought questions that require you to answer in a few sentences. You may complete your answers on the back if there is not enough space.

1. What did Hagar learn and how would this help members of your support group?

_____

_____

_____

_____

2. *What* job description did Jesus have and how does this affect you as a support group leader?

_____

_____

3. If you were checking the "lids" of your group members, *what* would you be doing

and *why*? _____

_____

_____

_____

4. A member of your group says, "I always feel so much shame when I pray." *What questions* could you ask that would help her get her "lid on straight"?

_____

_____

_____

_____

5. If someone says that coming to your group is like going to the beauty shop, *what would they be experiencing?* _____

_____

_____

_____

6. *How* will you know when your group members enter the "responsible" phase of change? _____

_____

7. As a support group leader, how will you apply Ephesians 4:12-16?

_____

_____

_____

LEADER'S WORKSHEET
SECTION TWO

To Know Yourself
Chapters 5-8

Your Name _____

Your Address_____

City, State, Zip _____

Telephone: Work (_____)_____ Hours _____

           Home (_____) _____

Aglow Fellowship _____

Section Two / PART ONE

The following questions require specific answers from the material in Section Two.

1. Confidence as a support group leader comes when you are sure of _____

_____.

2. Knowledge is not_____.

3. The book of Numbers gives us respect for _____

_____.

4. Under "Personal Leadership Qualifications," how many do you have in each category?

Ones _____

Twos _____

Threes _____

5. An effective leader must know both her _____

and her _____.

6. _____ is defined as the most basic part of you.

7. The Lord desires to transform our human nature by maturing the _____

_____

_____ in our lives.

8. Romans 12:6-8 defines what gifts? _____

_____

9. Where in the Bible are the manifestation gifts of the Spirit found?

_____

10. Life experiences make us _____

_____, or _____.

Section Two / PART TWO

The following are thought questions that require you to answer in a few sentences. You may complete your answers on the back if there is not enough space.

1. Reflect personally on Luke 22:32. In what way does this apply to your life and potential as a support group leader?

_____

_____

_____

2. Why would a board not approve someone to lead a group on grief if she were angry at God for letting her son die?

_____

_____

_____

3. You may have experienced help from or have knowledge of how other support groups function. What is your responsibility as an Aglow support group leader?

_____

_____

_____

_____

4. In what ways will this learning process toward Aglow's Certificate of Completion be of benefit to you?

_____

_____

_____

5. Name one strength and one weakness of your human nature: _____

_____.

How will they affect you as a support group leader? _____

_____.

Which fruits of the Spirit will help you? _____

_____.

6. Your primary motivational gifts are _____.

How will these affect you in leading a support group? _____

_____

_____

_____

7. Describe how you can expect the manifestation gifts to be used in support group?

_____

_____

8. Think about your own life experiences. How will they help you as a support group leader?

_____

_____

_____

9. How will embracing your essence make you a better support group leader?

_____

_____

_____

**LEADER'S WORKSHEET
SECTION THREE**

**To Know People
Chapters 9 -12**

Your Name _____

Your Address_____

City, State, Zip _____

Telephone: Work (_____)_____ Hours _____

              Home (_____) _____

Aglow Fellowship _____

Section Three / PART THREE

The following questions require specific answers from the material in Section Three.

1. Mankind's deepest needs are for _____,

_____, and _____.

Mankind's most common wound is _____.

2. A privilege you have in support group is to reveal the _____

and uncover the _____of the enemy.

3. List three types of longings: _____

_____

_____

4. Is the following statement TRUE or FALSE? (Circle one): Feelings are important and should be given authority in our lives.

5. God has not given us the right to_____

but the freedom to _____.

6. A father's voice has_____.

Listening to God's voice gives us _____.

Listening to man's or Satan's voice results in _____.

7. Support groups are places where _____takes place.

Change usually brings some type of _____ that people seek to avoid.

8. P-A-C means _____, _____,

_____.

In support group we desire to avoid _____messages.

List four common parental words you will try to avoid using:

(1) _____, (2)_____,

(3)_____, (4)_____.

9. _____ is a natural process of saying goodbye.

10. Forgiveness is a_____ we make.

    Unforgiveness is my attempt to be _____ .

Section Three / PART TWO

The following are thought questions that require you to answer in a few sentences. You may complete your answers on the back if there is not enough space.

1. A woman in your group does not feel joy in Christ, responds little to the Word, has a series of broken relationships, and carries much shame. From reading Chapter 9, what might you know about her?

_____

_____

_____

_____

2. Give an example of a "sin of self-protection" from your own life:

_____

_____

3. Sue shares with your group that her twenty-four-year-old son is constantly asking her for money that she can't afford to give him, but she doesn't want to upset him; after all, his father walked out on him and she is all he has. As group leader, using Chapter Ten, what might you do or say to her?

_____

_____

_____

_____

4. Explain how you will use your knowledge of the "Victim Recovery Path" in your support group:

_____

_____

_____

_____

5. Helen begins to complain that she came to your group to feel better, but dealing with her life is too hard and she's disappointed with the group. How will understanding "compound pain" help you help her?

_____

_____

_____

_____

6. Are you parental?_____ If you give parental messages as a group leader, what effect will this have on your group?

_____

_____

_____

How can you work on change? _____

_____

_____

_____

7. Ann's father abandoned her when she was eight. In her group she makes comments such as these: "It didn't affect me at all when my father left." "Some day, if I keep praying, I just know God will bring my father back into my life." What stages of grief is she experiencing?

_____

What feelings is she trying to avoid? _____

_____

How can you help her in group? _____

_____

_____

_____

8. Mary is bitter and frequently has migraines and depression since her husband divorced her. Explain to her in your own words the high price of unforgiveness compared to the priceless benefits of forgiveness:

_____

_____

_____

9. The ultimate purpose of all change for a Christian is _____.

   How will you encourage this in your group? _____

   _____

   _____

LEADER'S WORKSHEET
SECTION FOUR

Know Support Groups
Chapters 13-15

Your Name _____

Your Address_____

City, State, Zip _____

Telephone: Work (_____)_____ Hours _____

Home (_____) _____

Aglow Fellowship _____

Section Four / PART ONE

The following questions require specific answers from the material in Section Four.

1. Gethsemane was a garden for Jesus' _____.

2. Thoroughly defining our concept of support groups for Aglow helps us maintain

_____ and _____

in the ministry.

3. The leadership style advocated for your Aglow support group leaders is

_____.

4. Support groups should have no more than _____ members

   and should last no longer than _____.

5. It is beneficial to have an _____ leader

   and a _____leader for the group.

6. _____must be guarded if there is

   to be trust in your group.

7. Group _____should be read at every

   meeting. Leaders are responsible for _____

   and _____ them.

8. You are responsible to begin_____ and

   to _____, and to watch the

   _____ for each part of the group.

9. The outlines and check lists in Chapter 15 are not_____

   by Aglow, but are given as helps in keeping order and focus.

10. _____is a priority. Leading a group

   requires great giving of _____ and self must be

   _____ on Him.

Section Four / PART TWO

The following are thought questions that require you to answer in a few sentences. You may complete your answers on the back if there is not enough space.

1. Betty has seen your Aglow support group advertised and calls you to ask, "How is your Aglow group different from other groups and how will it help me?" Write out your answer to her:

_____

_____

_____

_____

_____

_____

2. Imagine yourself seated with your group. Explain to your group what your job is as facilitator and how that will help them.

_____

_____

_____

_____

3. Jane has appeared depressed for three weeks and today stated that twice this week she has looked for her husband's gun because her life is just too hard. What responsibility do you need to take for her?

_____

_____

_____

_____

_____

_____

4. Sharon has been argumentative and hostile in the group and has not responded to you in a personal talk with her. What should you do for her and for the group?

_____

_____

_____

_____

_____

5. How will you decide on material to use in your group? If you have decided on material, what is it?

_____

_____

_____

6. What role does teaching play in support group leadership?

_____

_____

_____

7. What role does prayer play in the group and for you as leader?

_____

_____

_____

_____

LEADER'S WORKSHEETS
SECTION FIVE

Know Your Skills
Chapters 16-20

Your Name _____

Your Address_____

City, State, Zip _____

Telephone: Work (_____)_____ Hours _____

　　　　　　Home (_____) _____

Aglow Fellowship _____

Section Five / PART ONE

The following questions require specific answers from the material in Section Five.

1. Your willingness to work at acquiring support group ministry skills tests your

_____

and your _____.

2. From Psalm 78:72 we aspire to _____

and _____ as leaders.

3. When you begin leading a group, use _____

   and_____

   to _____the skills.

4. Being "fully present" is an _____ skill

   that includes what you _____

   and what you _____ .

5. _____ is the primary attending skill

   and includes _____

   _____

6. A group leader must be _____

   _____

   _____.

7. You will "listen" for both_____

   and _____ messages.

8. With feelings, we want_____ and _____.

9. To help group members share and promote interaction, you use_____

   _____ and _____.

10. _____ are the primary probing skills.

11. "You said you were very angry," is an example of what probing skill?

_____

12. _____ problems in _____.

13. God will work through you if you _____

to the best of your ability, _____ Him

throughout the process, and sincerely _____ your group.

Section Five / PART TWO

The following are thought questions that require you to answer in a few sentences. You may complete your answers on the back if there is not enough space.

1. Each time you begin a support group session, the group will respond to the "quality of your presence" and the "skills of the heart." What are these essential elements?

_____

_____

_____

_____

2. You and your co-leader are checking each other's attending skills. What do you want her to see in you?

_____

_____

_____

_____

3. Patricia is anxious and has low self-esteem. What verbal and non-verbal messages have told you this?

_____

_____

_____

4. Laura says, "I need you to tell me what to do." What is an appropriate response?

_____

_____

_____

_____

5. Following the examples under "Types of Questions" in Chapter 18, give your own examples of each type of question using 1 Peter 5:7.

_____

_____

_____

_____

_____

_____

_____

_____

_____

_____

_____

6. "I had a really difficult week," June says. "I couldn't concentrate on anything and cried a lot. I don't know how much longer my family can put up with me." Using your probing skills, form two questions that might be appropriate and two statements you might make to this group member:

(Questions) _____

_____

_____

_____

(Statements) _____

_____

_____

_____

7. Marilyn is a dominator and Donna is a silent one. What would be appropriate ways to work with each in your group?

(Marilyn) _____

_____

_____

_____

(Donna) _____

_____

_____

_____

_____

8. From the chapter "His Final Touch," share your "final" feelings now that you have completed your worksheets.

_____

_____

_____

_____

_____

_____

_____

_____

Recommended Reading List

Aglow *Heart Issues* Books for Support Groups
Every *Heart Issues* book contains questions for support group and/or personal study at the end of each chapter.

Compassionate Care: Practical Love for Your Aging Parents

Caregiving for elderly loved ones (Aglow release, February 1994)

When Love Is Not Perfect

Reparenting for victims of childhood abuse, including sexual abuse

Friends Forever

The art of lifetime relationships

Who Says Winners Never Lose?

Recovery from a child's death and other painful life experiences

Beyond Fear

Overcoming fears in order to live fully

Jigsaw Families

Blending remarried families

If I'm Created in God's Image, Why Does It Hurt to Look in the Mirror?

Distorted self-concepts and new self-discovery in God

Daddy, Where Were You?

Healing for the father-deprived daughter

Lost in the Money Maze

Bringing godly order to your personal financial world (Written especially for women by a woman)

Sock Hunting and Other Pursuits of the Working Mother

Balancing work and family needs

(Special Aglow Edition)
Codependency

Published by Rapha. An excellent Christian sourcebook on dysfunctional behaviors and freedom from them.

Aglow's General Books

The following are not written specifically for support group use, yet they deal with the issues of our hearts and are used in many support groups.

Love and Its Counterfeits

Freedom from unhealthy ways of loving

How to Pray for Your Children

Basic strategies for upholding our children in prayer through good and bad times

How to Forgive Your Children

Applying the truths of God's forgiveness with our children

Healing the Angry Heart

The abusive Christian parent and how to get free

How to Say Goodbye

Working through life-changing grief from death, divorce

Grandparenting Redefined   Issues of grandparenting in this age of changing family structures

Books by Other Publishers

In addition to Aglow's material, the following books will help you more fully understand the issues and people in your groups. These titles represent only a portion of the vast resource of credible material available today. NOTE: *They are not all adaptable for group use* but are given as helps for your understanding.

Title	Author	Publisher

GENERAL HELP

The Search for Significance	Robert S. McGee	Rapha
Understanding People	Larry Crabb	Zondervan
Inside Out	Larry Crabb	NavPress
Lies We Believe	Chris Thurman	Thomas Nelson
Healing for Damaged Emotions	David A. Seamands	Victor Books

SEXUAL ABUSE

The Wounded Heart	Dan Allender	NavPress
Healing Victims of Sexual Abuse	Paula Sanford	Victory House

DYSFUNCTIONAL FAMILY ISSUES

Always Daddy's Girl	Norman Wright	Regal Press
Codependent No More	M. Beattie	Harvest House
Codependency, A Christian Perspective	Pat Springle	Rapha (Aglow Edition)
Love is a Choice	Frank Minirth	Thomas Nelson
Kids Who Carry Our Pain	Hemfelt	Thomas Nelson (Minirth/Meier Clinic Series)
Adult Children and the Almighty	Melinda Fish	Chosen Books

COMPULSIVE ISSUES

When Addiction Comes to the Church	Melinda Fish	Chosen Books
Love Hunger	Frank Minirth	Thomas Nelson

SELF IMAGE—DEPRESSION

A Woman's Strength	Annabelle Gillham	Wolgemuth & Hyatt
Happiness is a Choice	Frank Minirth	Thomas Nelson
The Anger Workbook	Carter	Thomas Nelson

OTHER

Fresh Start Divorce Recovery		Thomas Nelson
Love is a Decision	Gary Smalley	Word
The Marriage Builder	Larry Crabb	Zondervan

Source Notes

SECTION ONE

Chapter 3

1. Melinda Fish, *Adult Children and the Almighty* (Tarrytown, NY: Chosen Books, 1991), p. 25.
2. Ibid. p. 26.
3. Edwin Cole, *Maximized Manhood* (Springdale, PA: Whitaker House, 1982), p. 28.

SECTION TWO

Chapter 8

1. Mary Lance V. Sisk, "My Heavenly Father Is a Gracious, Loving Parent."

SECTION THREE

Chapter 9

1. Melinda Fish, *Adult Children and the Almighty* (Tarrytown, NY: Chosen Books, 1991), p. 55.
2. Ibid., pp. 96-98.
3. Larry Crabb, *Inside Out* (Colorado Springs, CO: NavPress, 1988), pp. 77-88.
4. Ibid., p. 132.

Chapter 11

1. Chris Thurman, *The Lies We Believe* (Nashville, TN: Thomas Nelson, Inc., 1989), p. 177.
2. Ibid., p. 183.
3. Elizabeth Kubler-Ross.
4. Timothy Foster, *Called to Counsel* (Nashville, TN: Thomas Nelson, Inc., 1986), p. 140.
5. Ibid., p. 137.

SECTION FOUR

Chapter 13

1. *Rapha's Handbook For Group Leaders* (Houston, TX: Rapha Publishing, 1991), pp. 4, 5.
2. *The Leader's Digest* (Lynnwood, WA: Aglow Publications, 1991), Section 8, p. 149.
3. Gerald Corey, *Theory and Practice of Group Counseling* (Pacific Grove, CA: Brooks/Cole, 1990), p. 65.

Chapter 15

1. *Right Step Facilitator Training Manual* (Houston, TX: Rapha Publishing, 1990), p. 124.

SECTION FIVE

Chapter 18

1. Gerald Corey, *Theory and Practice of Group Counseling* (Pacific Grove, CA: Brooks/Cole, 1990), p. 469.

2. Ibid., p 71, 72.

3. *Rapha's Handbook For Group Leaders* (Houston, TX: Rapha Publishing, 1991), pp. 28, 29.

4. Support Group Skills and Dynamics chart: The format of this chart is based on Edwin J. Nolan's article "Leadership Intervention for Promoting Personal Mastery." *Journal for Specialists in Group Work*, March 3, 1978, pp. 132-138.

5. Corey & Corey, *Groups: Process and Practice* (Pacific Grove, CA: Brooks/Cole, 1990), pp. 71, 72.